WHO
MADE
THE
LAMB

WHO MADE THE LAMB

By Charlotte Painter

McGraw-Hill Book Company

NEW YORK   TORONTO   LONDON

Library of Congress
Catalog Card Number 64-23637

First Edition

48087

For my mother
Dillie Womack Schmidt

Did he who made the Lamb
make thee?

—*William Blake*

WHO
MADE
THE
LAMB

PART ONE

A basket weaver here is making a cradle of straw. I stood outside his shop for some time today, watching him. The frame is complete, though not yet put together, and is in two parts. The one, a simple rectangle, will become the bed, to be suspended within the other, a supporting base. Rather than rocking, the bed will swing from side to side, away from the base and always on the same level. Thus, the baby will not be thrown off balance or jerked about, as I imagine could occur in a cradle set on rockers. The weaver fitted a tan straw covering to the frame, and while I watched he finished it with a brown and tan border of Indian design. It is a pattern used in much of the straw furniture made in this part of Mexico, and matches a chest of drawers in the weaver's shop. The man looked up at me finally with a formal smile that turned humorous. Or perhaps that was my fancy. Surely he couldn't guess that an American woman who stopped to admire a piece of his work had necessarily some use for it.

—*Muy elegante, Señor.*

—*¿Le gusta, Señora? No es cara.*

In his doorway was the little boy we have befriended, playing with some younger children. We think that he himself must be old enough to go to school, for whenever we pass him he calls out, "George Wash-ing-ton," and grins with secret knowledge. We have begun to return his greeting with "Beni-to Juár-ez," and that causes him to shriek with bliss. We can get nothing more out of him. He goes shy the moment we try to expand the range of our communication.

The weaver's hands have such large knuckles you'd think they'd get in his way as he braids the straw. Probably the children in the doorway are his. He could be making the cradle for himself and may have offered to sell it to me simply out of habit. Though on second thought he probably could not afford such a luxury. Neither can I, but I want it and am sure to show it to Tom. Then there'd be no question: we would buy it.

For some days I have found my husband looking at me with a dazed, private wonder, and then realized the expression reflects my own. We laugh. Can it be true? Perhaps not; it could be something else.

We are sure. What else could it be? But American to the bone, we look to the verdict of the specialist. Should we go home now, a month sooner than we planned, or await a further sign?

Often, I sit in our tiny patio on the stone stoop beside an old tiled well. The colors are strong and bold. Shoots of green thrust up between the stones of the patio floor. The vines that twist up the wall send tendrils with magenta and yellow blossoms around and over our three doorways, which are painted a true red. The russet-red tile roof slants up toward a cloudless blue. And there, the sun gives out light that subdues the glare of all this gaudy show. The sunlight of Mexico is gentle and suffused, steady but thin almost as the air. My own feelings shed more radiance: I am with child, I am with child. I feel I've taken in all the color above and about me. I am deeper than our well can possibly be. I rest my head against the tiles of the well, for an immeasurable time.

It is only the time in my reverie that is immeasurable. For time in the patio is always short, because of the infestation of flies. There is no getting rid of them. They mob the unpaved streets. They are the most active life in the village. And besides, it happens that our rear wall separates us from somebody's barnyard. We wonder how the hotels down the street keep out the pests, but courtesy prevents our asking, even though our landlady owns one of the hotels. Insect spray is a best seller in the drugstore, and the señora who runs it has made us a present of a *bomba* of Flit, which is effective for a matter of a few blessed minutes. Nevertheless, the flies intrude upon my thoughts only long enough to drive me into the bedroom, where I go on dreaming in the shuttered light.

If it is really true, then I have cast my lot with the rest of womankind. There are certain things about our sex I cannot easily understand. How is it, for example, that we for so long insisted on a right to share in the conduct of life, and yet so willingly exclude ourselves from taking advantage of that right and don't like to look upon it as a duty? I shall come to motherhood rather later than most. Perhaps many things that a young girl might take for granted will baffle and surprise me. Perhaps this experience will tell me something about the nature of women that I have not understood before. Those of us who have deferred having children because of work or other causes are aware of some tacit, secret bond among mothers. We have wondered at their own often eager separation of themselves from their husbands at a party, and have not doubted there was more to it than a distaste for male talk. What can its meaning be? Is it a universal instinct or just habit, this secret bond? Whatever it may be, the distinction is even more noticeable here in Mexico than at home.

Perhaps a woman ought to be living in another culture when she learns she will bring a child into her own, for a better view of the life she has to offer that child. Our child will inherit a geography that spans our continent, from Tom's adopted San Francisco to my adopted New York, and if that isn't enough we have our desert and deep-South breedings to toss in. And because we must travel a great deal, the child will know our particular taste for the exotic. As well as our particular xenophobia, for, like most people abroad, we feel ourselves more American than ever. And here we are more reflective about the things at home that we deplore. What we deplore has become more real, a possession of our own. The Latin who blames our country for the hydrogen bomb and the social miseries of his land blames us personally. And so we find ourselves pondering responsibility. And I wonder if women, mothers in particular, have been derelict, or have undertaken as many of the hard tasks of the world as their nature allows.

This is a village in which to consider women and their nature. We noticed almost at once that it is a place of women. Mexico City is close enough to draw away the young men, who can find little to do in this tiny spa. The modest tourist business cannot support them and has, to judge by the quiet deterioration of the hotels, seen better days. That is not to say the town won't enjoy a revival once it becomes a suburb of the capital, as it inevitably will with the spiral of industry from the center. But for now, many of the hotels are owned by women, as are the drugstore and the grocery store. It is the women who sell, who govern, who beg. You can actually trace several centuries of womanhood within a single village block, too, from the old mothers with seamed faces who sit upon the curb outside the hotels wrapped in their stoles, to the café owner's young wife, a career-minded former divorcée of infinite resource. We are surrounded by a complex of primitive, medieval, and modern cultures that make our own monotemporal world at home seem less of a puzzle. Our predicament is singular, alike to all: it ought to yield to some easy solution. But here I think I find more access to primary human drives than at home. Like primary colors, they are allowed more open use. In that sense, there is greater simplicity.

The old women of the curb prey upon the patrons of the hotels, mostly Mexicans from Mexico City. To the beggars, Tom has only one thing to say: *"Somos pobres."* I thought that heartless at first. Obviously, we are rich: we go to a hotel to swim afternoons; we wear shoes. It is even said that the man is a professor at a university in the United States. That is doubtful, since he claims to be only an *antropólogo*, a considerably lesser status to the experienced Indian. So many Indians have served as informants that, in one state at least, there are jokes that anthropology is the third biggest industry after oil and beer. The fact that Tom is not doing fieldwork now, but writing, as I am, makes us all the more suspect. For writers always drink to excess, as everybody knows. The old women murmur together when they see us, but whatever they feel they keep inaudible except for the word they direct to us: *"Tan-ti-to,"* an economy that approximates: "Give me just a tiny little bit." As soon as I got to know the town, my Puritan heart hardened with shocking firmness to these weird sisters, for other old women have honorable occupations. They roast corn upon a grill beside the curb, or squat before pyramids of fruit in the market square.

I have befriended a woman who roasts corn, and she has promised to bring me some seed for *cilantro,* which is a delicate, parsley-like herb used often here. Tom says I must be sure not to offer to pay for the seed but to buy corn from her instead. She has unusual eyes, bright blue, set in a gleaming, ruddy face. Her hair is completely white, but she is lacking only one front tooth. She found it very amusing that I wanted *cilantro* seed, and beyond belief that we did not have it in the States.

All the medieval women here are made to look like comely shades by their flowing stoles, *rebozos,* most of which are navy-blue cotton flecked with white. Even the little girls wear them with a grace, not at all clumsy or coy like children playing ladies. It is their everyday dress, after all. Babies you do not see, even though the national population is very much on the increase. You know there must be babies and that in most cases they must go where their mothers go. And then you remember the *rebozo.* To be sure. It is not a mere adornment, but a carryall. That is often a chicken or a turkey thumping inside the shawl, but sometimes the flap and coo may be a baby's, not a fowl's.

One of the twentieth century women is going to show me how to carry a baby in a *rebozo.* She is An-

gela, the café owner's wife. I asked her as we were
leaving last night, and she said she would demonstrate
when we came back tonight. Nothing had been said
about our coming back tonight, but that is Angela's
way of drumming up trade, which is slow enough
here. They serve an Arabic coffee (her husband is an
Arab immigrant) and a Mexican brandy, for which
they overcharge us outrageously. But we enjoy talking
to them, and so we shall go back tonight.

There is something I like about Angela's method
of getting us to patronize the café. It isn't candor in
the sense Americans understand it, but it admits of
no deceit. Our landlady, whom everybody calls Señora Mona, also has this amiable way of serving her
own interests with great hospitality.

She and her eldest daughter, Elena, were among
the first we met here. We had been directed to knock
on the door of the hotel owner's apartment, only to
discover that the door opened onto a bedroom and
that two ladies were taking an afternoon rest on the
twin beds. The older woman urged us to enter, explaining as if by apology that she would not have invited us to talk business at her bedside if we were not
Americans. We had been to see the several houses
that she had for rent. Only one was furnished, and
we told her that with certain minor alterations it
would suit our needs. These alterations were in the
nature of work space, for the tables in the house were
inadequate.

Good—good; everything would be arranged to

suit our taste. Señora Mona rose and, pulling her *rebozo* about her broad chest, said she would go with us and see just what was needed. Elena came along, as did two boys who worked at the hotel. Señora Mona, said to be the richest lady in town, entered the house and began to lift object after object. Would we have any use for this chair, that tray? In fact, no, we like a bare look; and so piece by piece the boys bore off much of the furniture. The two front rooms were extra bedrooms, she said. They opened onto the patio and could each be locked individually. We were only two and would surely have no use for them. She would simply store some of the furniture within and lock them off from the rest of the house.

It was Elena who came to our rescue at last. We needed tables, she reminded her mother; she could not lock those up. And the boys must bring some others, some better ones. "And, no, Mama, they must have the best bed. It is one thing to close off two rooms, but the best bed must be moved into the bedroom they are to use." Elena went on with a gentle pressure until at last her villainous mother gave a good-natured laugh.

"Didn't I say you would have everything to your taste? And because I like you, I will have something special sent here to the house. An icebox. That will make your kitchen quite complete." We had not counted on such a luxury, but Elena assured us there was one standing idle in the hotel kitchen. In the way. Admirable Señora Mona, woman of affairs. Everything was indeed arranged to our taste. And to hers.   9

Tom has been outside in the courtyard for a while, sitting with a soft, bemused gaze. I know that he is thinking of me.

Hope possesses us like a strong spell, and that too sets us apart from our neighbors here. Being human, they surely hope, but with such modesty as to heat the extravagant American heart with a touch of anger. A lady from a tourist bus scolds a ragged beggar child for not being in school. She means only that her hopes outweigh the peso he is hoping for. And it is the children who disturb her more than anything she sees here, for somehow the little "drop of seed" provokes the strongest and most unreasoning of human visions. Hope, on which cosmeticians and fortune-tellers, as well as more vicious sinners, thrive, is potent magic. It can distort reality for us beyond recognition, can turn us to an acceptance of strictures of religion and politics that reason easily refutes. It can induce us to disregard experience and discount character. It deceives us and defeats us. It even disguises itself in philosophic robes of despair, so that modern thinkers may embrace it without apology. But it is not all black magic. It also enables us to survive unkind conditions and to transcend ourselves on the peaks of the possible. There is little wonder I think of it now as a strong spell, which also contains an inseparable antithesis: fear. We cannot hope deeply without fear, and today our hopes are as large as all creation. . . .

She looked up at me, the lady who roasts corn, and shrank back in an astonished movement that seemed to say: I thought you would have vanished as gringos always do. She had not brought the *cilantro* seed. She laughed. Tomorrow, tomorrow she would bring seed. She had forgotten. I hastened to tell her that she needn't worry about it, for she looked very much ashamed for doubting me. I said tomorrow was time enough—in fact, next week or the next. We plan to be here for some time, I said. She smiled and smiled, not believing me again.

Tom has gone out now to look for the iceman. It is a daily excursion. Señora Mona's icebox has stood empty since its arrival, for no iceman has appeared. He comes here, they say, from a neighboring town on the main route to Mexico City, but either he has not received the many messages we have left for him or he has not had ice to spare us. Meanwhile, Coca-Cola is served cold everywhere, and because bottles in the stores are surrounded with beautiful ice, we know he has passed through. We are probably the only Americans within a thousand miles who have rented a house and tried to run it without a maid. Perhaps we are resented for this. There never seems to be meat left when we go to market, or even tomatoes, which are plentiful everywhere. A maid could save us this trouble, find us ice, and manage much better in the inadequate kitchen. But we are stubborn.

The rapidity with which our lives are changing is a continual surprise. Only a few months ago Tom took me to "the hill." His private place. That stretch **11** of California public land high above town, a forest that held deeply hidden glades. Someday it will be a park, but now no one goes there. At least, we never saw a soul there except ourselves. He wanted me to have it, too, because he knew I needed a place private from all others, a retreat, a secret place. The first time he took me there and left me in a clearing, it was like a gift. He could wander off with some solitary puzzle of his own, and come back for me later, for there was space enough for each of us to trouble deaf heaven or to praise it. Sometimes, of course, we shared the place. We would speak of ourselves in the third person then. "They," often celebrating something, packed picnic baskets with wine and tramped through the woods, or along the Pacific shoreline, always within sight but usually too absorbed by each other to notice "us" dogging their footsteps.

I imagine this division of ourselves would pose no challenge to those who believe that reducing character to its lowest common denominator is a way to explain it. Obviously "they" are caused by an anxiety over pleasure drives. The split-off frees "us" of responsibility for "their" acts. But we (or they) prefer less parlor science and the greater latitude of nature.

To love a complex nature unreservedly, to see the complexity as neither trial nor threat but a source of enrichment and renewed delight, is an uncommon gift in a man or woman. Perhaps all of us may be born with it but cannot retain it in a world that is itself so complex that our very survival sometimes depends upon the use of simplifying ideas. We want the simple

life, we say, simple relationships. And we forget that
the only simple human relationship possible is a shal-
low one. Our life here in Mexico has many simple relationships. If I buy corn from a street vendor, there
is no difficulty at all. Money and corn change hands,
and perhaps even a few friendly words are exchanged,
but nothing disturbs the peace of my complexity or
fosters it in any way. But see what happens when I
ask for more than the vendor has: *cilantro* seed. Then
something interesting goes on. Imagination, memory,
curiosity are quickened, and the thing is already so
complex that weeks go by before it can be dealt with.

No, I believe that when we say we want a simple
life we are confessing to a deep longing for the power
to deal with what we are, and to enjoy what we have
inside ourselves. It is true that some people are helped
by shedding external trappings. Houses, cars, property, and bank accounts encase them like armoring,
and they cannot even begin to breathe until they get
loose. But the simple breath of life should not be confused with the complex experience of it.

Today he has come! The iceman's truck is in
front of the house. Except that he is not an iceman.
He is a beer man. His ice is completely free, but available only to his beer customers. If we buy a case every
week he will bring us ice every day. We hesitated: we
don't drink beer. Then we added it up. Beer is a soft
drink here; a case costs little more than we might expect to pay for the week's ice. In a matter of moments
that cold commodity that warms the hearts of Amer-

icans everywhere stood in the box, and a case of beer stood beside the well in the patio. The ice-beer man asked us to pay for the beer but not for the bottles, which are worth as much as the beer. He will collect them when he brings our next case. A most trusting extortionist.

We won't go to the café after all tonight, because the rain has lasted longer than usual. Most days, it ends in the late afternoon. From Tom's studio, which is really a maid's room over the kitchen, we can see it begin. The clarity of the sky goes suddenly, and with it the surround of dusty green hills. And then the clouds close in on the town in a circle, until at last they billow like purple blankets over the pink church dome at the square.

Tonight we shall work, if our neighbors permit it. We know a great deal about our neighbors, although we have never seen them. She is named Julia, and her husband and brother-in-law are the village drunks. They have begun to pound on the gate again tonight. This happens about twice a week, and causes their dogs to howl. A howl here has the concentric action of a pebble tossed into a pond: it makes widening circles of sound about the town until every dog has joined in. "Julia, Julia!" the husband calls, begging her to open up. At length, she begins to scold from within, often refusing the men admittance, whereupon they pound and sob and the dogs howl for hours. Tonight, perhaps because of the rain, she has been more merciful to us all.

Something about Julia reminds me of a neighbor in my childhood, a stern, reproachful matriarch, bearing her cross a little more noticeably than necessary. And other women here, too, bring back the world I grew up in, as it was then. Mrs. García, who takes in washing, ours included, uses a scrubboard and tubs in her backyard. Gentle-faced and decent, she has seen to it that her daughters have a better life than hers. One of them works at Señora Mona's hotel as a secretary; the other has just been voted Queen of the Lions Club. And the daughters—Mrs. García's, several of Señora Mona's, all the teen-age girls in town —one feels they all hope to become movie stars. They dress elaborately for this small town, wear spike-heeled shoes that make them stumble on the cobbled walks, and tease their hair into styles shown in movie magazines, as if they see themselves as their generation's María Montez or Dolores Del Rio. One grass widow runs a guesthouse, while her husband keeps a backstreet *casa chica* in Mexico City. And there is even a gold digger from out of town who snagged the only rich American. I wonder if the nation's Sinclair Lewis or Fannie Hurst is not quietly at work in some corner of the town.

Sometimes I think there is indeed such a thing as a time machine.

The baby in the *rebozo* is a simple trick. In the absence of a baby, Angela used an empty wine bottle to demonstrate. First, she draped the stole about her shoulders, with one end a good bit longer than the other. That is the part that contains the baby. Then she slung the bottle inside, as if into a hammock, gave the end a twist over the "baby's" feet, and brought the opposite end around to tuck over the "baby's" back and bottom. That way the mother's hands are left free for whatever chore demands her attention. The drama of this use of the *rebozo* is that the under-piece is supported in place by the weight of the baby, not by any knot or fastening.

I told Angela that I had seen a little girl of twelve or so wrap up her little brother against her chest, making a knot at one end of the shawl, and Angela confessed that it gives more security that way but is not correct. She passed me her stole and bottle, assuring me that it was very easy. Indeed, nothing could have been more so. One quick twist, wrap, and the wine bottle lay smashed upon the floor.

My cultural resistance is considerable. I wonder about the curiosity of a child who lives in a *rebozo*, for it can't look out. I prefer the North American Indian backpack or the Japanese harness, either of which allows the baby to face the same direction as the mother for a view of what she's up to. (The chances are that I shall settle for a stroller, though.) Even though the fabric of a *rebozo* is porous and admits quite enough air for breathing, I imagine a set of annual statistics: *Year's Rebozo Infant Fatalities.* And newspaper headlines: *Another Rebozo Baby,* or *Mother Smotherer Jailed.*

Angela is an actress, dark-haired, fair-skinned, and very animated. She has lived in Mexico City and

16

worked in a few television plays. With an uncle, she is now rehearsing a play that will tour the provinces. But she is not single-minded about her career. The café murals, which give the place a North Beach flavor, are from her brush. She tells me, too, that she has written a one-act play. She is also working on a handcraft exhibition, a bazaar for the village square. Unlike many middle-class Mexicans, she appreciates the value of native art, even though her purpose is to exploit it for sale to Americans. She believes no money can be earned here without a knowledge of English, which she is teaching herself for want of a tutor or classes here.

As we were leaving, she asked, "But I hope that you are not—do you say 'embarrassed'?" This is a reference to my interest in the use of the *rebozo. Embarazada* means pregnant.

I wonder, is a pregnant woman embarrassed or an embarrassment? Unlike our own, the Spanish tongue has choked on the Latin root and come up with a free association. Most intensely personal terms seem to have been too embarrassing even for that to English-speaking people.

And why, I wonder, did Angela hope that I was *not* "embarrassed"? Anyway, that hope, together with a certain sharpness in her tone, was enough to prevent my confiding in her. I told her I thought not.

Tom has just come in to say that he has seen a very handsome cradle in the basket shop down the street. A swing, woven of tan and brown straw. So . . .   *17* he has found it himself. How virtuous I feel not to have mentioned it. But nobody uses cradles nowadays, I said. They are outgrown too quickly. And besides, we may not need it. Then, too, we have enough to pack in the station wagon as it is. But we'll go to bargain with the weaver one day soon, we have decided.

How ignorant I feel. And, at moments, how utterly childish. There's so much I want to know, and there's no one here to ask. Angela? But how would she know? She must be as ignorant as I. Mona? Yes, I could ask the señora, for she has four other daughters besides Elena. But the thought gives me an acute fit of shyness. Over the weekend we went into Mexico City, where friends could have suggested a doctor, yet I did nothing, confided in no one. We went into Sanborn's, where I found on the paperback bookshelves a copy of Dr. Grantly Dick-Read's *Childbirth Without Fear*. Fear is not at issue, though. I feel no pain, no difficulty; rather, a light-headed elation all the time. The truth is, I don't want to *know* yet—I might be disappointed. And so how can I say that fear is not at issue?

This morning I went with Angela to see her aunt's little house, whose charm she did not want me to miss. The charm consisted mostly of its bath. No ordinary bathroom, it is set over one of the hundreds of warm natural springs here and is the size of a railroad car. Long and narrow, walled in with brightly colored tiles, it is worthy of the noblest Roman. All

18

the hotels here have these little private pools—we use one of Señora Mona's every day—as well as large outdoor pools, and Angela says that many people like her aging aunt have them, too. The waters are said to cure everything from arthritis to impotence and sterility.

A curious thing happened as we were starting out from Angela's house. She was talking to me, as always, in a bright, vivacious stream of Spanish, when she suddenly interrupted herself. "Juana, Juana!" she called in a shrill tone. From the corner of the square, her maid, who had been talking to someone there, came at a run. "We're going now," Angela told her. The maid nodded and rushed into the house. Without another word to the girl, Angela stepped outside with me and locked the door behind us. She saw that I looked puzzled. "In the United States they don't lock the maid inside when they go out?" I told her no. This news she was promptly to share with her aunt when we arrived. "Imagine! Carlota doesn't lock up her maid." I very much doubt if maid-locking is really a widespread practice, but Angela insisted that at least in this town it is the thing to do. "They might take away your whole house one day and never come back."

I have heard it said that this is a nation of comedians. Perhaps that is because the people think it would be undignified to disguise the part of their nature that comes from the fox. Both Angela and the maid accept the imprisonment as a necessary precaution, given the human animal. They don't notice (or *19* care) that this acceptance excludes the hope of change. That too is what makes for comedy.

The old lady of the *cilantro* seed and I have talked again. She keeps forgetting the seed, but seems so genuinely apologetic (as well as surprised) each time she sees me that I hesitate to drop the matter. I could easily go to a seed store when we are in Mexico City again. But one day she will bring her seed and would be disappointed if I didn't show up. Her blue eyes shine with an intense desire to please.

But sometimes the women here drive me mad with their servility and cowardice.

Scene: the grocery store. A new clerk, a young girl with a tender innocence in her light brown face, looks up as the American couple come in. The man is carrying a rather large shopping bag filled with a dismaying number of empty bottles. These bottles have contained soda water, Peñafel, but now they do not, and the Americans have just asked her to pay them for the bottles. For so many? She stares. It seems impossible, what they ask, but she will try to deal with it, as the señora is busy in the back. She asks, Did I sell you the Peñafel? She has sold several *refrescos* that morning to people in the neighborhood who later came back for their deposit. For each empty bottle she knows she must return fifty centavos. But this is a different situation. There are so *many* bottles here. Eight, perhaps. No one else in town keeps so many bottles, for who has so many *tostóns* to spare for so long? Perhaps these bottles are—no, not stolen, there are no thieves in town, but perhaps they are counterfeit. Yes, perhaps that's it. She lifts a bottle gingerly from the bag, taps it against the display case, but it holds firm. No bubble that, but glass. She looks at the Americans dubiously and shakes her head. It is not possible that any honest person could have so many bottles.

The American man makes a move to go, but suddenly the American woman is seized with a sort of stubborn fit. She tells the clerk either to give them the money or to make a note of what is owed. She says she doesn't want to buy groceries just now because she isn't going back home right away. Still the clerk is puzzled. She talks too quickly, this American lady, and seems unreasonably annoyed, almost as if she might feel guilty of some sort of cheating, even though she is clearly rich. The last thing she has said proves her wealth: she has carried the bottles here just to get them out of the way. Out of the way! The deposits would mean nothing to her, and yet she insists upon them. Is it possible she knows they are equal to a good part of the clerk's wages? Is it possible the American woman knows she may be *depriving* the clerk of her wages? What a vexing puzzle she is! And now she has turned to her husband with a look of sheer exasperation, although he would be happy to leave. Very well, there is no help for it but to call the señora, who comes with a smile.

Ah, the Americans. They are such good customers. The señora quickly counts the bottles, and orders 21 the girl to give the Americans four pesos. Everyone is greatly relieved. Then a look of doubt crosses the señora's face, and she intercepts the money on its way from the clerk's hand. Did they really buy the drinks from her store? Perhaps when that other clerk, the boy, was there? Ah, that explains everything. That boy was unreliable. She had had to let him go. He was to blame for the terrible avalanche of bottles. With a smile of cheerful resignation, she allows the deposit to change hands. That boy, yes. Men! No wonder. They are to blame for everything.

We have survived another week without a visit from the iceman. The beer, however, is being drunk by another American resident, a writer. He once enjoyed some little celebrity, but has not published in many years. He is the kind of writer, in fact, who confirms the native opinion of writers. He lives in Mexico because a bottle of gin may be bought for less than a dollar here, and rum is even cheaper. He speaks no Spanish. That deficiency seems to make some Americans assume a fraternity with others that does not necessarily exist. Tom is more humane than I am and will not withdraw from those who are dependent in this manner. The man knocks at our door at any hour of the day or night. I have suggested that he and Angela exchange language lessons, to give him something to do other than call on us. Of course, I feel ashamed of myself, for he is lonely, but I am hard with resolve. It is difficult enough to use our best energy here without its being consumed by our misplaced countrymen. We react badly to the altitude. We wake each day as if drugged. At home we swam half a mile a day without effort; here after three laps in Mona's pool we are gasping. We often have the impulse to pack up the car, and flee.

In the café tonight, Angela was making a costume of Aztec design, which she said she planned to wear to the benefit. This is to be a big affair in the garden of the town's rich American, and the proceeds will go for a recreation park for the children of the village. I asked Angela if we could attend without costumes. "To be sure. Only those who are part of the program will be in costume." That made me assume she would be in a performance of some sort, but when I asked her about it her manner became mysterious and, I thought, somewhat defensive. Then she refused to talk about it altogether.

People came from several towns for the benefit, and some of the entertainers even came from Mexico City. The hotel people were out in full force—the guests, the two elderly men who own hotels, and all the ladies, several of them without an escort in this town of petticoat rule. Our Mona came with her oldest, privileged daughter, Elena. The storekeepers came, the lady who gave us the Flit bomb, the grocer lady, and another lady who runs the mercantile shop. Such people as Mrs. García, the laundress, were not there, **23** but her two daughters came. All the shop and hotel owners are members of the International Lions Club, to which anyone of any consequence belongs.

The dance floor was the sundeck beside the swimming pool, and the orchestra played behind the pool. On the other side, behind the guest tables, stood refreshment booths. For the most part, they were set up by the hotels, each booth contributing a hotel specialty—*tamales, tacos, chiles rellenos, dulces*. But the last booth gave me a start. Angela was sitting there in her Aztec costume, selling Arabic coffee. This was a considerably smaller role than I had imagined her to have in the entertainment, and it explained her evasiveness of the night before. She sat in her Aztec costume, a pretty picture of discontent. She should have been a part of the floor show, and here she must sell coffee and tell fortunes. Some of the entertainers from Mexico City would do a "genuine" Aztec dance.

At the booth, the Arab, usually very cheerful, was grumbling about business. "As the last in the row of booths, we will not sell much coffee," he said. Word went around that Angela was telling fortunes from the coffee dregs, but even that didn't seem to help much. "I'm sorry we bothered," he said, and Angela agreed.

With her was her uncle, the actor with whom she had tried her luck in Mexico City. He kept trying to adjust her feather headpiece, which often slipped from place. There was such dissatisfaction in her face that after we had taken a table I went back to talk to her, to try to cheer her up. I reminded her that it was early yet for coffee, that few people had even begun to eat, and asked if she'd warm up by telling my fortune. And so she filled my cup, I drank, and she peered into the dregs.

We were interrupted then by a surprising incident. A child of about five, a little girl, came up to the booth and, without a word, as if she were quite familiar with Angela, turned her back so that Angela could see that her sash had come undone. After Angela re-tied it, the child said, *"Gracias, Mamá,"* and vanished into a group of other children. Angela glanced at me, I thought with a certain furtiveness, and then seeing that nothing had escaped me she said, "My little sister." But to make sure, for she could have confused the English terms, I answered her in Spanish. You mean your daughter? No, she had made no mistake, she said; she always called the child her sister. People thought she was too young to have a daughter; it might interfere with her career.

For a moment I felt myself in that time machine again. A generation ago, actresses in Hollywood were said to do this sort of thing, but no more. It would be thought silly nowadays, if not immoral, for a woman to conceal her motherhood.

Now my face gave me away, I think, for Angela returned to a study of the dregs of my coffee, embarrassed. I could never find a man more suited to me than my husband, she told me. I asked her if the dregs told when I would have a child. She pretended to think it over, and asked for my birth date. When I told her, she grew more lively, for I shared the same sign as she. The twins! Ah, that explained a great deal. "You want a child and at the same time you do not. You are that way. You often believe in something and at the same time disbelieve. Want something and do not want it."

It isn't true, I thought, and was at once unsure. Why had I refused to tell Angela the other night of my hope? Was it because it was a dread as well? But no, Angela herself had discouraged my confidence, seeing motherhood as a restriction, just as now she was assigning to me her own mixed feelings.

She sat at her coffee booth in her feathered Aztec headdress, like some bright caged bird of a buried age, longing to soar into a life from which she was exempt. I thought of one of Camus' rare philosophical references to women, where he argues that a passionate woman necessarily has a closed heart, for it is turned away from the world. It seems to me that American women are capable of refuting such a view as that. Angela, of the American continent, but in her passions closer to the European women Camus spoke of, is separated by many years, even centuries, from most of her own countrywomen, and we find her heart at a turning point. The world her heart turns out toward may be narrow and frivolous, but it is larger than the solitary cell of the self that imprisons so many moderns, and it is not bound by a circular maternal passion.

Indeed, I wonder if Camus' passionate woman doesn't tell us more about a certain male vision of life, in whose range biology is a mere charade, where close and enduring affections are seen with the eyes of the mock hero Don Juan: men live in groups; how nauseating, how absurd! No, I turn away from such a gloomy, unrejoicing gaze. It cannot endure for long the face of love without knowing revulsion. Nor can it even envisage a woman with child. And so fearsome a trap is passion that it cannot see that a nature such as Angela's admits virtue as well as folly.

In weighing ourselves against other women of today's world, we Americans ought to accept a handicap, for other women must treat with such matters as have been made obsolete for many of us by modern history. Women (and men) have alway been meretricious (and how often that flaw is wed to industry, as in Angela's case). We can't really admire Angela for being alert to opportunity, for we can't admire her aim. However, we can see that scarcity of opportunity restricts her. She must seize the chance that passes like a merry-go-round ring—while we others are surrounded by such an abundance of choice that we hesitate, linger over decision, and often fall into idleness or discontent. To reject a false view of life is a relatively easy exercise. But to get about the task of selecting a meaningful pattern for our lives is infinitely difficult. That is the handicap of plenty.

Angela next looked into my palm. Suddenly she gave my hand a tight squeeze. "Oh, I was wrong. There is already a child on the way." She smiled in encouragement, surrendering to her nature's other side. "Never mind any doubts. It is worth it; it is the best thing."

A copy of Montaigne is on my shelf next to the book we bought in Mexico City, *Childbirth Without Fear*, and I've been sampling both tonight. Montaigne's mistrust of medicine was deep and well founded. How little the temper of the medical fraternity has altered in our favor since his day! He said, "Whatever Fortune, Nature or any other extraneous cause produces that is good and healthful in us, it is the privilege of medicine to attribute to itelf." Since normally a child is a good and healthful thing, I believe a patient owes it to herself to take on what responsibility she can for what occurs, Nature and Fortune permitting. So does the author of the other book, a revolutionary, as all pioneers probably must be.

I remember now the passionate partisans Tom and I knew in New York and San Francisco who insist on childbirth without anesthesia, and would like to learn more. Any system that will permit me to invade territory usually proscribed except to doctors will be of interest. I try to remember what the partisans said, and can't. Their concerns had struck me as rarefied then, as if they were to live for a time in some interplanetary state, at a remove from the matters of this world until the pregnancy ended. It may have been caused by their own remote look, but I can distinctly remember a sense almost of taboo toward a pregnant woman: leave her be—she's not quite of this world. Perhaps if we look at it honestly, the elaborate deference we pay the pregnant woman may be an inversion of some ancient taboo. I think there is no doubt that she suspends for a time certain mundane preoccupations, trivial ones perhaps, and is thus indeed placed at a remove from the matters of this world. That would be enough to antagonize us; but not liking to admit it, since new life is necessary to the race, we adopt a romantic view of considerate deference for an interesting but not pertinent condition.

As I was reading, the dogs began. Tonight there is a full moon. At about midnight Tom went around to see if he could quiet the dog at Julia's, for nobody seemed to be at home and it was howling incessantly. He had no sooner left than there came a thud on our roof. These walls would be very easy to scale, but the only prowlers in the village are cats. They crawl onto our balcony and scavenge around our courtyard at night. As cats go, they are very heavy-footed. For some reason, even though I knew the sound, I felt a little apprehensive. Then, when a knock came at the door, my heart gave a short leap. Tom had a key. I went to the front without turning on a light and stood listening for a moment. *"Quien?"* No one answered. Then I could see the stole of an Indian woman in silhouette at the window, and I opened the door. She worked for the American, the writer, she said. He had sent her to look for Tom. Would he come, please? She gripped her baby tightly. I asked if something were wrong, and in a rush of confidence she said that the writer was very drunk, worse than usual, and crazy too. That he had taken her baby and tossed him up into the air until he hit his head on the ceiling. She got the child away from him only when he began to scream with pain. Tom crossed the street from Julia's and told the girl he'd go back to see if he could quiet the man. I knew that the maid had a sister, and urged her to go stay at her sister's house for the night. The thought seemed to terrify her. She had not even allowed it to enter her mind. Even though I promised to explain that it was my idea, she was too afraid of losing her job to act on my advice.

Now the dog at Julia's has started up again. I have just tried to shout at it to shut it up. However, it is very difficult to say *"perro"* properly in a loud, commanding voice. The *r*'s vitiate the vowel when they are trilled. At least, my efforts were ridiculous. The dog didn't respond, and I sat down on the bed, dizzy from the effort. Something jarred inside, and my abdomen burned. I've always heard that one must be careful in the first six weeks of pregnancy. Why was I such a fool as to lose my temper over a dog? But of course it wasn't just the animal that made me angry. I am out of patience with *all* this—howling dogs, prowling cats, ever-faithful flies, deadbeat Americans, anachronistic women. I want out, *out!*

I realize now that the book about childbirth I had been reading, intending to reassure, had frightened me. And sometimes I react to fear that way, with anger—especially if I know it is a fear that can be dealt with. The frightened woman who has just left could have dealt with her fear had she been able to use my superior know-how. And I? The science of genetics offers me *its* know-how: two cells have united and multiply, building upon each other. The result is inevitable, unalarming, identified. But genetics does not yet explain the mystery it identifies, the mystery of new life. And so ... I shrink into my *rebozo*.

The cradle is gone. The basket weaver has sent it to a town on the route to Mexico City to sell it in a store there. It is just as well. We don't have room for it. But I feel sorry because the weaver was so obliging. His brother had a truck, he said, and could go get it for us from the shop. No, there was no time, we said, for we were leaving tomorrow. He told us he could make another and ship it to us in the States, and so we have taken down his name. I doubt if we shall want to face the bureaucratic morass involved in making such a shipment from here, however. We bought some baskets from him and said goodbye to his little boy, who was playing outside the door. "George Wash-ing-ton," he said.

Just as we were leaving, we remembered the ice-beer man's bottles. What should we do with them? He had not shown up for more than two weeks. The bottles from his last delivery stood in the patio, emptied by the American writer, now locked in a room at the village clinic. We had left the key to our house at the hotel, and could perhaps leave the bottles there for the ice-beer man. But at the hotel we could find no one willing to assume responsibility for them. Mona and her daughters had gone out for the afternoon, and the porter was afraid someone might steal them. We went to the grocery store, but the señora was out. The young girl there turned quite pale when she saw us enter with the case of bottles, and was unwilling to listen to a thing we said, merely shaking her head and saying we must come back when the señora was there. Now what? we asked each other. Oh, leave them in the patio, we decided, outdone. But then, as we finished packing up the car, a solution presented itself.

"George Wash-ing-ton," said the little boy from the weaver's shop. He and half a dozen other children stood agape, watching us. One or two remembered to ask us for a *quinto*, but what we were doing was so fascinating that it was more fun to watch than to beg. When the car was ready, and the motor warming up, Tom went back inside and reappeared with the case of bottles.

They went wild with joy as we passed them around. One of the smallest was so excited that he promptly dropped his, and they smashed on the sidewalk. But the occasion was too great for tears. He looked up at us, and grinned. Oh, wonder of wonders, the kitchen yielded two Peñafel bottles to replace the broken ones. Nobody waited now to wave goodbye, as they had surely planned to do. By the time we were settled in the car, the children were far down the block. They had at once run to the grocery store, and we could hear the beginning of a powerful argument with the girl behind the counter. Oh, remorseless Yanqui capitalists!

We drove down to the square and stopped for a moment at the café to say goodbye to Angela and the Arab. She came out to the curb with us, and just as we were driving off we heard somebody calling, "Señora, Señora . . ." It was the old lady who roasts corn, and whose station is adjacent to the café. Her bright blue eyes glowed in satisfaction when we stopped, and I went back. She dug down into the pocket of her apron and came up with two handfuls of seed. *"Cilantro,"* she said.

I transferred the seed to the pocket of my dress, thanked her, and walked back with her to her grill. "Is there corn?" I asked. No, she had sold all her corn that day, she said, again with a gratified smile. How sad I felt. I had nothing for her, and could not even buy her corn. I searched my mind for something more to say, some way to show my appreciation, yet nothing came. The space of several centuries blocked me, just as surely as they have removed me from a dedication to the matter of the old woman's life, constant worry over the essentials, food, shelter, clothing. Yet, in her satisfaction with the two successes of that day, selling her corn and delivering my seed, I could see the common ground of women through those centuries: she grew and prepared sustenance; she nurtured seed. We will not give it up, whatever material or idealistic gain we make, for that is how we can maintain the pulse of life.

When I returned to the car, Angela laughed. "She's a very good woman, that," she said. Then we all waved goodbye.

PART TWO

With Tom at the campus, I stare at the telephone on the kitchen wall, nervy and surprised at what I am thinking. I wish that *he* would do it for me. Finding a doctor in a strange southern city will be no easy task, but it is nothing I am unequal to. I have always, by choice, managed such things, and now . . . so much of my prized independence is slipping away from me.

We are only partially moved in. The shipment of books and the household clutter are yet to come from California, but we have found a place we like. Out of step with the world as usual (which here does not walk but drives upon the asphalt of a hot valley overhung with smog), we have withdrawn to the nearby hills. The city sends up fumes that don't reach this countryside, but at night they suffuse the depression there with an orange, infernal glow. As solitude becomes harder to attain, the hills everywhere remind us that we still have a choice. Life need not be a flat congestion if we don't mind living out of sight of other people and have no fear of heights. But even these hills are becoming densely populated. There are several subdivisions close by, and the owner of this property has sold her frontage to developers. Soon this area, half an hour's drive from the campus, will be swallowed by the city corporation, and water lines will go down and that infernal orange glow will spread into the hills.

But as it is, we drive up from the pike on a private road onto the hundred-and-fifty-acre tract, past the tall farmhouse to our cottage, a remodeled barn. Our water is piped from the springhouse below the cottage. It also feeds the small pond adjacent to it, which one of Tom's colleagues has already derisively dubbed our "Walden Pond." I wish it were, but the pond is a sluggish mudhole, its bottom easily measurable. However, between the springhouse and the pond there is a little rivulet where watercress grows every April. And over the hill a larger lake yields bass to occasional fishermen who come in response to the sign at the road's entrance: *Drummond's Park—Closed on Saturday.* (Why Saturday? I must ask.) We would cheerfully forego the pond and move to town if Concord lay below us, but unlike Tom's colleague we cannot resign ourselves to living in a house with mock Doric columns or even within sight of such a house. That is the order in his neighborhood. We concede that our prejudice against the southern Greek influence is at least as strong as his against nature, and there let it rest.

The false columns are more prevalent here than in the deep South that I grew up in, most of them being of recent construction and directly influenced by an inspiration of the city fathers, the Parthenon. This Parthenon was completed just over thirty years ago. It was built on the flattest part of the valley, and excepting its site emulates in concrete that marble temple on the Acropolis. It is regarded as an imaginative tour de force by the citizens of this "Athens of the South." Perhaps they know of Thoreau's dream that Concord might become a kind of Athenian city of universities, where men of goodwill and learning might freely enjoy a feast of reason and a flow of soul. If he lies uneasy in his grave at what has come instead to Concord, perhaps his spirit should have a glimpse of this southern interpretation of that vision. At Christmastime a department store erects a giant crèche before the columns, possibly as proof against pagan worship. I have only driven past and haven't seen it close, for fear that more may yet be learned about this matter of prenatal shock.

The archaeology of the rest of the town is equally interesting, if less sensational. In a generation of industrial sprawl and spill, the new has merely been superimposed upon the old, a city built on top of a little town. Overpasses mesh and twine above streets grown too narrow for the traffic. The ancient station house, sooty and decrepit, stands in a state of near abandonment beside a six-lane highway, and will one day be swallowed by it when the eighth lane goes down. Government buildings crowd against a bend of the river as if in danger of being shoved off by the press of traffic surrounding them. On the map, the valley is like a battered bicycle wheel, the spokes the main streets, all crowded highways in fact, for a throughway bypass won't be finished for at least another year. Commerce pulls the people in and pushes them out, and on weekdays they drive furiously back and forth along the spokes. The hub of the wheel is a barren place like New York's Wall Street on Sunday, as desolate as any Aztec ruin. We rode the spokes our first few days here. Most cities prove to have some charm for us—in a waterfront, a park, an architectural line. Even New York's wasted Wall Street has some terrible beauty in its height and shadow. But here, nothing reaches up impressively, and the only cooling shade we have found is in these hills.

Tom is a "visiting" professor, which is a reassuring title to me. At first he joked: he "teaches primitive religion and evolution in the Bible Belt." But he has already found, even on this most high-toned of southern campuses, there really *are* students who have Darwin linked in their minds with Judas.

There is so much I cannot tell my husband about this monstrous, engaging, hypocritical, friendly, vicious South. He knows that it differs and how it differs from the rest of the country, but he knows it only in his head, and that is not where he is vulnerable.

Here, of course, we must align ourselves in our nation's race war, a commitment which may be conveniently deferred in some parts of the country—for the present. Many manage to defer it here, to be

truthful—many of both races. And for both, polite-
ness and apathy perpetuate an inferior standard of
life, like that of a cripple who refuses an operation
that would enable him to walk for fear of the surgeon's blade. To delay personal commitment out of
the belief that it is not a personal concern, is to ignore
wilfully the existence in man of the conflict between
good and evil. There are many who would always
deny the urgency of treating with that conflict—on
pain of eventual bloodshed.

Tom came home for lunch, and was surprised
at my obstetrical report. After talking to various medical societies and half a dozen doctors or their nurses,
I had found one obstetrician who agreed to discuss
delivery without anesthetic. We had made an appointment. The usual guide in such matters was not
yet available to me—the Underground of other patients. And the medical fraternity guards its integrity
so closely that one might suspect that its alchemy may
not always withstand inspection. I might have been
asking for someone to bleed a fever or prescribe a
voodoo sack for colic, for all the blanks my queries
drew.

"Go to a woman," Tom said, and I had to tell
him there was not a woman obstetrician within a
hundred miles. He believes it is a job women should
excel at. But his faith is evidently not shared by the
medical profession. Or by women themselves, perhaps. Tom's esteem for women is, I've found, higher
than their own self-esteem.

And then he thought of the solution that, in our fumbling ignorance, we had overlooked. The university medical school must have an obstetrics department that must at least pay some attention to upstart ideas, if only to be conscientiously modern. I decided to keep the appointment already made but to call the university if the interview was not encouraging.

He was quite paternal, and his tolerance made a sharp impression on me. He told me many of the difficulties a professional man must deal with in the variety of women who come to him. I had an opportunity to observe some of them for myself during the two hours I waited in his outer office. Most of them were young girls whose conversations with each other were marked for the most part with a contented ignorance of childbirth and a faith in the doctor that bordered on hero worship. One said: "He's marvelous. He'll put you out and you'll never feel a thing." Such passive acceptance bothered me, and so I had to ask myself why. The very title of the book, *Childbirth Without Fear*, which thousands of women have read, *presumes* fear, and humans react to it in different ways. A desire "not to feel a thing" is only one reaction, an awfully timid one, I thought.

Then I eavesdropped on another conversation: An experience in a delivery room, vividly detailed, was recounted. The girl had a beautiful face, but memory masked it with a strange anger. She had failed to react to the anesthetic given her. She was conscious throughout the delivery, in severe pain. But the over-riding emotion of her story was rage. She kicked the obstetrician, she clawed the nurse, she cursed, she even stormed out of the room once before she was captured and bound to the table. She explained that she was now having tests made to ensure better re-sults with her next anesthetic, for she too wanted to know *nothing,* to feel *nothing.* Yet she talked of her earlier experience, of the nurses, the interns, the accommodations, with an intense fascination and complete recall. It was hard to believe she left out a single detail of that experience she so wanted to be unaware of! Was it possible that what she really wanted was to avoid her own anger? She ended her story with a flat assertion: "I'm not afraid; I just want to be sure that this time I'm *out.*"

I realized as I sat there that in wanting to give birth without an anesthetic, to see our baby born, I was in deep. What instinct was at work in me? Is this fear of childbirth peculiar to women alone, one that men cannot experience, no matter how well they may ameliorate it? Given that fear is one of the great-est limiting forces known to humans, we might con-sider whether women are more limited than men, and if so whether fear may be the cause. We give our anx-ious thought to matters that men will often dismiss as inconsiderable. Who hasn't seen the flicker of im-patience in a man's face before kindness persuaded him to reduce a worried woman's mountain of con-cern to a molehill? "My dear, if it *does* rain, it's only a picnic." And what is behind her desperate worry about rain? Questions of security? Men worry, too, whether the sky will fall, and have built enormous stockpiles of arms to allay their fears.

Surely both sexes fear separation, death, destitution; but men and women have long behaved differently about such fears. Appeals to gods and the creation of institutional safeguards are more in a woman's line, but a man prefers traditionally to take some action. Out yonder in the hills his prey abides, which will provide sustenance for his family. He fears it, but advances toward it, and if he is not eaten himself, his fear is cast off in a triumph of achievement. He can then return to the hearth and say, "Woman, I have prevailed."

Women have taken advantage of no such reprieve. They have not advanced toward their fear and come to grips with it in a symbolic survival struggle. And so strongly is this difference in behavior felt that women who concern themselves with acts of survival invite criticism. A safari huntress and an aviatrix may be game but they are also odd. I have even read that a woman who wants to take part in the birth of her child must want to prove herself a champion and that such a desire is not natural. And yet to me it seems perfectly natural to want to enjoy a triumph of achievement. Why should that be only man's province? We do not forbid him to worry about the weather forecast if he likes, but we may think him too timid in his choice. Such timidity, the limiting force, has historically been the recourse of women who have confused it with modesty. It is possible to be both modest *and* bold, although as Abigail Adams said of the perfectibility of human nature, it is sad that "our admiration should arise from a scarcity of instances."

I made no effort to explain these thoughts to the doctor when I was at last admitted to his office, for I became too interested in what he was saying. I lay beneath the careful folds of white draping provided by his nurse, while he probed and spoke. I am not, he assured me, unusual. Many women read articles. Books, even. The difficulty appears to lie in our acceptance of what we read as gospel. We forget to take into account that our doctor has read not only our smattering of information but a great deal more. This experience, so new to us, is not at all new to him. He frequently delivers three babies in a single night. He moved with firm gentleness and took a case history with admirable speed. His blue eyes gazed at me with the assurance of a man accustomed to trust from the Frail Vessel.

As I sat across the desk from him afterward, he made a church of his hands, and smiled. There's one thing my article hadn't told me, and it seems I might better have played bridge the day I read it. He said that any woman of my advanced years must have a Cesarean section. And here is how he hastened to deal with the resistance he saw in me: "Of course, your husband being an anthropologist, you may think all you have to do is go behind a bush and give a few grunts. But you're not a native, or even a European.

You're a well-brought-up American girl, southern to boot. You're used to a modest, sheltered life." Modest or timid? I wondered.

Well, what was not down on my case history was certainly in his heart. His good intentions were unquestionable. But he was not talking to *me*. "Why, they don't even drape the women in Europe, you know," he said. And he spoke of the ease of Cesarean delivery, the benefits to both mother and child, the security of setting a birth date rather than enduring the ordeal of labor. "Childbirth can be a very violent thing," he said.

I started to be difficult and tell him of a friend who had delivered normally at forty, but then I decided to let it pass. After all, I *am* southern bred, and courteous. And if I had begun to pick at his method, I might have asked him about all the elaborate swaddling I had undergone before his examination, and wondered just for whose peace of mind it was intended. It is barely possible that *he* may find it more comfortable to have his modest southern gentlewoman out cold at the moment of delivery. It may be painful to a man, if not downright embarrassing, to see a lady do a hard day's work while he just stands by to help her out. I might have suggested that having this baby was my business at least as much as my doctor's, perhaps more. But breeding will out. The Frail Vessel left him in command, and paid the toll for his half-hour on her way out.

I also paid for my restraint, however, and came home unutterably depressed. Perhaps it wasn't restraint but cowardice. Perhaps I should have insisted on what I wanted.

Some previous tenant had a garden patch in the acre beside our cottage, but now it has become a field where the Drummond dogs chase rabbits with tireless futility. The two smallest dogs, a black Pekingese and her single hybrid offspring, a puppy of six weeks, have a particular liking for that field. The stubby-legged Pekingese can't keep pace with the puppy, whose legs have a miniature racehound elegance. She clumps after him eagerly, until he loses his rabbit and chases back to tumble her instead.

I consider again my notion of the nature of fear in women. The great majority of American women may not admit to it—fearing nothing, seeing no challenge, suffering neither longing nor ambition. It well may be that those seductive pictures that look out at me from the woman's page—the lady in Dior, the lady with the tasteful antiques, the lady in her habit astride her noble steed—may represent the best we are and all we should aspire to. Privilege and ease, freedom from conflict. If they did not bring so much discontent, perhaps I could desire them. And the discontent, doesn't it often come from the failure of awareness? The conquest of fear aside, at the event of a birth, it should not be difficult to see awareness as desirable, a prized quality. I want to know what is to happen to me. If someone we love dies, no one offers us an effective anesthetic until our bodies have absorbed the shock. It is an experience of our lives, to be felt, absorbed, used, if we have the wisdom to do so. Birth and death bear close resemblances.

Tall growth is kept down in the field outside by an abundance of wild morning-glory vines. They mesh and twine flat against the ground, yielding silken cups of purple and crimson and translucent white with broad blue veins. That fantastic early-morning acre, glowing and damp, becomes a garden of the dead by noon, the petals closed and withered like cut flowers on the bosom of a vast grave. And then the next day's dawn and their renascence, until the reiteration of the hours seals them up again. Ladylike flower, open-centered only to the dewy hours of life, oblivious to the loss in each day's overthrow, thriving on diurnal mockery of death.

"Come and get some of these greens!" Mrs. Drummond shouts out to me every time she sees me, pointing to her vegetable garden behind the morning-glory field. We see her only when we go to our car, which is parked near her back porch, for she has some difficulty with her legs that prevents her from walking much. But she urges us to her garden whenever she sees us approach. She has greens, okra, corn, peppers, and crowder peas, all grown with organic fertilizer.

Mrs. Drummond has inside her what Mark Twain has called a memory machine, which releases the record of her life in an uncensored flood so that the listener has the difficult, if not impossible, job of sorting out the relevance of events.

Today I accepted some greens, and asked if I could pick some for her as well. "No, Billy Ned's got ours already," she said. Billy Ned is a hired hand we met the day we came to look at the house. He was waxing the floors at the time. Billy Ned would, she told us then, take up the linoleum from the floors if we didn't like it, and wax and polish the boards beneath, and he'd clean out the oil heater and scrub down the wood paneling of the walls. He had, she said, just painted the outside of the barn white and the roof green. He seemed delighted to learn about these new duties. His adjustment to her benevolent tyranny is silence and obedience, but everyone is silent with Mrs. Drummond.

A widow, she is a tall, large-boned woman, with quite handsome features and a gravity of face that is dominated by immense gray eyes. The grayness of her appearance, however, does not withstand the contradiction of her merriment. She is driven, and constantly amused. Formidable.

When I had picked my greens, she shouted out again: "Now, you come here into this house. I want to show you something." Her old country kitchen has every possible modern convenience: washer and dryer, two deepfreezes, two refrigerators, food choppers, liquefiers, mixers—the works. She opened a cabinet to show me a great variety of health-food herbs. She began to fill a small jar with a fine yellowy powder. "Now, you take some of this—we have to fight them every whichway, you know. We have to

47

fight for our lives, with what-all they're putting in the
ground and in the air to poison our food with. You
are what you eat, you know. And if you eat that poison, your very heart will be a poison to your body and
venom to your loved ones."

She had believed she was waging a lonely war
against the chemical industry, and was astonished
when I told her that in California we had bought
nearly all our fruit and vegetables from a very success-
ful stand supplied by farmers who used no chemical
fertilizer whatsoever. A naïve wonder touched her face
for a moment, but then she sighed. "Ah, California,
but that's the other side of the mountains." For a
moment it seemed all that mechanical clutter in her
kitchen was just an illusion, that vast stretches of
wilderness had yet to be penetrated, that some new
Donner Pass must be crossed and absorbed by the
conscience before the land of milk and honey might
be claimed. But then when I told her of the organic
food farm run by my friends in Bucks County, Penn-
sylvania, she became greatly excited. "We're gaining
on them, you know. They'll lose out, even before the
Day of Judgment. *They* bear the mark of the *Beast*,"
she declared. Who? The ones who are poisoning our
land and polluting our air.

She began to speak of her own travels, her winters
at Miami Beach, her loathing—positive loathing—of
the town in the valley below, to whose citizens she
has sold real estate, sewing machines, religious ency-
clopedias, and other necessities. I began to edge toward the door. If I were going to follow her recipe,

I must get cracking, I said. It takes hours, I said, clutching her bottle of yellow herbs.

She followed me onto the porch. A car had pulled up outside, and a young girl got out and ran up the steps. She would have been pretty except that her silver-blond hair was black at the roots. Her manner toward Mrs. Drummond was evasive, I thought. She brushed past us with only a brief greeting. A man behind the wheel touched his hat to Mrs. Drummond, turned his car around, and drove down the gravel road with a rude screech of tires. Mrs. Drummond took my arm and went down the steps with me.

"Did you see that? Her arm?" I had noticed that the girl's upper arm was bandaged. "It was a tattoo," Mrs. Drummond whispered. "I'm having it taken off for her. She's from the prison, you know." I shook my head; I didn't know. They tattoo girls in prison here? No, no, it was a very long story, but she didn't hesitate to tackle it. The girl, Dorrie, had been in prison when Mrs. Drummond was a missionary there. (And so I learned why Drummond's Park is closed on Saturday, the Seventh Day.) Mrs. Drummond had persuaded the prison authorities to let Dorrie out on parole, in her custody. The man who had just driven off was her parole officer. She said: "I wanted to give her a chance, she's so young. But that *tattoo!* First I went to see a surgeon. I couldn't take her in with that tattoo. It was the name of the man who got her in trouble. It was a brand for life, I told her, if she didn't get rid of it. She agreed. This is her fourth operation."

For some reason Mrs. Drummond wanted me to understand clearly her feelings about the tattoo. It was a very strong revulsion. She gripped my arm. "It made me sick," she said, "that such a young little thing bore that Mark. Somehow I couldn't look on it as the mark of Cain. If I could, it wouldn't have cost me so much money. We all bear the mark of Cain. It's invisible, but we all know it's there. No, it seemed like that girl was bearing the Mark of the Beast. It seemed like if I could just get it taken off of her, then she might one day get so she could choose the other way. I wanted to see that girl's arm *clean*. She couldn't ever choose the Mark of the Lamb as long as she had that tattoo."

It stopped my retreat, that flow. She folded her hands and glanced off into the hills briefly, then fixed me with a fiery eye. "The day will come when we all must choose," she said. "Dorrie doesn't know it yet, but we have a wonderful Saviour."

I followed her instructions precisely with the yellow powder, bouillon cubes, and herbs, and we have eaten the greens for dinner. They were perfectly delicious.

Robert Graves insists that religion, "to deserve the name," must be prophetic, and that in America prophetic salvationism has all but vanished except in these very hills. Mrs. Drummond lives what she believes. No wonder she is driven. And constantly amused.

In this adventure in the world of medicine, I am impressed by the disparity between the professional man and the scientist. A professional man can probably inspire confidence more often, for he deals with people more than with facts. He may even have the cunning (or the wisdom) to conceal his blind spots, unlike the professional I saw the other day. The integrity of the "real pro" (as he is called in some circles) is concerned with meeting the standards of his trade; the scientist with meeting his own standards. I have now placed myself for good or ill at the mercy of a scientist's integrity.

"No, not on the basis of age alone," he said of the Cesarean prognosis. "Many women in their thirties have considerable flexibility. We don't know enough yet about the aging of cells to make categorical judgments of that kind."

I myself had made a categorical error in arriving late, based upon my two-hour wait at the professional's. Here there was no waiting room, only a chair in the secretary's office beside a shelf of books on gynecology and obstetrics. But there was no time to sit down, for the doctor had been waiting for me.

"The aging of cells." It had a coldly inhuman sound. This doctor has a high forehead, and eyes made both large and distant by bifocals. His extreme height has induced him to walk with a slight stoop. He is so lean that somehow I suspected his slender hands would be cold to the touch. He lectures when he talks, but watches, too, for affirmation that he is understood. He weighs his student and talks neither up nor down. "I haven't the style of the medical man who can take the little lady's pulse, prescribe something, and have his mind on the next day's fishing trip," he told me. He is droll, I thought, and felt immeasurably relieved. "In fact, I often catch myself using academic jargon to patients. You'll let me know, I hope, if my explanations aren't quite clear? It's a result of teaching more than I practice."

As head of the school of obstetrics, he has a full teaching schedule. He prefers to take only cases that might have some bearing on his clinical research in fertility. Although he knows that my pregnancy began with almost indecent promptness after my marriage, my "aging cells" might cause some difficulty in conceiving in the future. It is perhaps of interest. Or at least I could see he hoped it might be. Otherwise, my blood pressure could as well be taken by some member of the golf-and-fishing set. Then, too, there was the inquiry I had made about childbirth without anesthetic, probably one of the few such he had had since he came here from California. "Now, what books have you read?" I told him, and he suggested two others.

If I had wanted a partisan, I had not found him. Although he believes his science has made a great advance with recognition that the mother can take an active part in the birth of her child, he said: "We have a long way to go. Natural childbirth, ideally, is rather like making a Rolls-Royce. Each step calls for dedicated supervision and absolutely perfect raw materials." He didn't belabor the metaphor. It sufficed to explain one reason for medical resistance to natural delivery: prohibitive costs to both hospital and obstetrician. A man would be hard put to make three such deliveries in a single night. Then, too, there is the woman in the case. I thought: I probably don't present absolutely perfect raw materials. But I would like a Rolls-Royce baby. I told him I wanted to try. He added, "I said *ideally*. In practice we modify the precepts for American women, as you'll see in the book I've recommended." The sacrosanct American woman again. What is so special about us? I wondered again: Is such modification for the benefit of the women or of the doctors? Perhaps as I go along I'll find out.

Another disadvantage: If he isn't likely to be delivering three babies at the time mine is born, he may possibly be absent altogether. Lectures. He studied his calendar. Yes, he had two speaking engagements in my "due" month. But he will work with a consultant. Still smarting from the shopping around I had already done, I asked him to suggest someone. He said he would have another doctor at the hospital see me later on.

The "professional" doctor had assured me that confidence in one's doctor was most important, and I'm sure he was right. Perhaps he was right about many things. He is obliged because of competition to "keep up with new experiments," and has the arduous task of scanning the vast amount of technical mate- **53** rial printed every month. That alone is enough to make his impatience with an uninformed lay view understandable. But medicine as a business is one thing; as a vocation it must be quite another.

The doctor with a vocation must retain some of the classic virtues of scholarship—humility in knowledge, indifference to wealth, an unwillingness to use or reject new methods on the strength of authority or influence alone. My professor of obstetrics explained that his patients pay the university, which in turn pays him a salary, that his contract with the university permits him to accept no fees. If I detected a certain ruefulness in his tone, I nevertheless prefer his form of commitment to the professional's. His hand was cold, as I had expected. He is distant. Often we find that the laboratory search can cause the flesh to chill. An open heart and an open mind don't necessarily go together. For all I know, too, my doctor may have a more frivolous hobby than the pursuit of the golf ball, and as part of the modern university system he is compelled to work with a dilute version of the classic scholarly virtues. But he has a vocation, and that is what it takes to inspire my confidence. I left him elated by a sense of hope.

I told Tom of one of the doctor's moderating remarks: "Pregnancy *can* be a time of well-being like no other—for some women. But the pleasure is not in carrying the child, you know, or delivering it, but in having it as a mother." It seemed a rather melancholy view for an obstetrician. He helps create a new life, and yet his tie with that life is broken when he cuts the umbilical cord, when the best part begins, I said.

Tom laughed at this idealism. "You don't understand," he said. "Pregnancy is not regarded as a process of creation. It's a disease of the uterus."

Tom is very happy that the doctor has promised to waive the hospital rule and permit him to be present in the delivery room. He wants as much as I do to feel this entire experience as something that is peculiarly ours. I think that is rare in a man. Rather, I believe few men can give in to such a desire. Tom is incapable of clamping down on his feelings and adopting a conventional perspective. How *we* are, together and in what we do, is the most important thing in his life—that is his perspective.

Last night I wore my first maternity dress to a party, causing at least one man to expound with elaborate sentiment about "the most beautiful time of a woman's life." An unashamed romantic.

Then later another romantic made a puerile remark about Tom's war experience in Korea. "A man *needs* a war," he said.

While both remarks struck me as silly, they must have a basis in the goals we set for ourselves. I notice that women talk about their childbearing experience in much the way men talk about combat. Perhaps childbearing and warfare both suggest some violent hour in which we either justify or fail ourselves. *Childbirth can be a very violent thing.* When we

55

think of war, our first association is combat, not the drudgery of discipline, the monotony of waiting, the fatigue and strain of a long march. Perhaps child-bearing is like that. And then, the women who tell me their outlandish and wonderful confidences seem to have something profoundly important at the back of their minds, as if for a little while the Answer had been tight in their grasp but had somehow got away. Perhaps warfare is like that, too.

Elvira. Maid-of-all-work from the center of town. She came today to help me unpack the shipment from California that had at last arrived. Because Elvira is from the deep South, and moved here only last year, a persistent servility clings to her, endowing her with a personal obligingness and dependence, those dying qualities that white Southerners grieve about losing. Elvira is young, though, and will throw off her servility. She is already capable of recognizing that I am no older than she and may be looked at squarely in the face and called by my first name. With a little education, she might one day come to consider me an equal. She is the mother of four children, however, and so it is doubtful that her natural curiosity will ever receive more formal instruction than it has already had. She is small, a size seven, but she sews and is glad to have my cast-off twelves. She has a half-gold tooth in the foreground of a generous mouth. Her wide, wondering eyes contrast agreeably with the iron-ness of purpose I discovered her to have.

"That man drank," she said of her husband. And

so she had saved enough to move here. She could not have managed that except for a female relative in a similar situation with whom she now has a mutual child-care arrangement. Geographical mobility is very difficult for people like Elvira who care about their family ties, a fact that some social reorganizers don't take sufficiently into account. But Elvira means to be mobile. "I'll get enough ahead again to go to Chicago or Detroit or some place," she said, "to get away from that welfare crowd they have here."

Naturally, I wanted to know about the welfare crowd, and while we unwrapped my dishes, washed and stacked them, she explained. The story was like a fable and began with its moral.

"People are just naturally greedy, and the Government don't know what to do."

She said, "They have the same thing 'down there.'" She nodded southward. "It's the neighborhood that needs to get broken up. Let me tell you how it is. 'Down there' they have to be married now to get the checks. So they get married as soon as they get pregnant. Then the husband leaves, and they can prove nonsupport and desertion, so it's like not getting married, know what I mean? Some of them don't know the father, and don't care—that type. They get a bigger check every time they get a new baby. They don't work because if the welfare lady finds out, they stop the check. They can't make more than the check no matter how much they work, anyway. So what happens is the same as here: they stay home, and they get pregnant again, and they don't

57

do anything but gossip and drink. And if I say to them they can't ever get anything ahead this way, they say I'm no better off and look how hard I work. . . ."

I questioned these sweeping remarks, and she said: "Not *every*body. Listen, the vast majority are like you and me, know what I mean? But these are the ones that bug me. My kids might grow up and marry their kids, don't you see? That's why I got to get out of there. *My* little girl might marry one of these juveniles they're raising." She meant "delinquents," I realized when she mentioned them again.

I asked her what she thought such women were afraid of, and she looked bewildered for a moment. "Them? They're tough. They're not afraid." She was silent, thinking it over. After a moment, she shook a coffee cup by its handle. "Yes they are, yes they are," she said with sudden conviction. "Let me tell you about Kate. This neighbor, she got found out. Just like the rest of them, she lay around waiting for her check. Her house was filthy. She left diapers every whichway, and slop all over the kitchen. Well, they found out her husband was still coming around and living off her checks. A lot of them do that, but get away with it, mostly because they just show up at check time. Well, they stopped the checks on Kate, and she got scared, all right. But you think she went out to look for a job? She wasn't *that* scared. She started on the starch. That's all."

When Elvira learned that I had never heard of the folk addiction to cornstarch or laundry starch, she could not believe her ears. "Good Lord, everybody knows about that!" What I said next must have sounded awfully sententious, I realized: "In Mexico there are Indians who gorge themselves on clay tablets as a religious duty."

"Duty!" Elvira cried. "Not these people. They eat it to cut down on their appetite. Then they get so they can't stop." Her fable continued. One day she went to visit Kate and found a box of starch on her bedside table. Elvira urged Kate to stop eating it, to sell her television set instead. But Kate wouldn't listen. Elvira went to speak to the grocer. "He's a white man, and it's not his fault. He says that when he sees them buying more than usual he tells them he's out of it." She took some groceries back to Kate's and cooked dinner. Kate promised to reform. However, a few days later Elvira heard the television set blaring and the baby bawling, but no answer came to her knock. She walked in and found Kate in the bedroom.

"She had a box of that starch, and she say her neighbor give it to her. She had a spoon in her hand and she was feeding it to the baby. And him no more than six weeks old. She put it on the spoon handle because that baby's mouth was too little to take in the ladle, and it was sucking with all its might. I asked her how long she been giving that baby starch, and she say it's the first time, but I could see it's had a lot because its belly's all blown up." Elvira said that she took the baby away from Kate and was keeping it at her own place.

A sense of unreality made me dizzy. I sat down.

Elvira was washing glasses in my bright country kitchen. There were fresh red- and white-checked curtains at the window and a matching tablecloth before me. The artifacts of our time were there—mixing bowls, pepper grinder, ovenware, skillets. I reached for a skillet handle to hold onto until my balance was restored.

Elvira said, "If the government was smart, you know what they'd do?" She does not confuse native intelligence with education, and is quick to see that the educated bureaucrat often acts under the mistaken belief that learning ensures his intelligent behavior. Elvira would cut through the conflicting interests that plague the welfare program by the simple expedient of tyranny.

"Work camps," she said. "That's what they ought to put those girls in. Instead of waiting to put their *children* in reform schools when they're juveniles. Make them go to school for a year and learn how to do something besides lie on their backside. Make them learn birth control. Then afterward, until they can get a job, make them pass a house inspection before they collect their check. If they live free off the country, why shouldn't they have to be at least as clean as the rest of the country?"

I told her that probably more than one half of the country's elected representatives, particularly those with the greatest welfare constituency, would simply laugh at such a notion and that the other half would see justice in it for the wrong reason. "What wrong reason?" she wanted to know. And so I tried to outline some of the abuses possible in corrective education, in imposing moral standards in a free society, but she soon looked very tired.

The racial conflict doesn't bother Elvira much. Her children go to an integrated school. She said, "The Government can do something about the violence. Violence isn't always bad, anyway. But why don't they stop people from being lazy and greedy, and, like you say, afraid?"

I had run out of answers.

Violence isn't always bad, anyway.... I wish I had asked her what she meant. It had no reference, I know, to Negro schoolchildren who might be stoned, to lynchings, or even to the long history man has of finding ways to condone murder. She puts more faith than she knows in "the Government," even as she deplores its helplessness. What she *is* fighting appears to be the old tautology that poverty and its accompanying deadly sins are always with us, the comfortable conviction that helps maintain poverty. She wants nothing less than to put our natures to the test of a psychic mutation. Whether the species is capable of such a change is not yet established, some say. The record speaks against it. Yet we change within the circle of a family. Until a child learns the early lesson that the cost of love is the sacrifice of greed, he doesn't become quite human. With Elvira at the center, I can imagine emanations of conscience seeping outside that closed circle, spiraling out, to do violence to the deadly sins of greed and sloth. And if that is only a pretty fantasy, perhaps she ought to

join the "crowd" she so despises. I would hate to
have to break it to her.

Our baby has all its features, except nails and
teeth. It also has a long tail. And if it is female, it already has a womb. How quietly it grows.

The starling migrations cause an uproar among
the dogs. As soon as a sound like locusts announces
a flock's decision to perch for the night upon a certain
tree, the coon hounds, the Spitz, and the two tiny
black dogs protest ferociously. It is the same whenever a car comes over the hill, and sometimes visitors
will wait for reassurance from their hostess before
alighting. But not these birds. Their noisy roosting
probably makes them oblivious to the landlocked
creatures. It happens several times a day—the barking, the chattering, a rustle of painted leaves. And
when the leaves are settled on the burnt-out ground,
the dogs subside.

The sense of property possesses the puppy, too,
at three months. Because walking is prescribed, I
make a daily excursion to the mailbox on the pike,
half a mile away, and the mother Pekingese and
whelp come along. The first day they followed me,
the next they ran ahead of me, and now it is established that when I come out in the mornings it is
to take them for a walk. The puppy resulted from a
union of Tarbaby Chihuahua from across the pike

and Babe Pekingese, and is an unusually happy genetic
outcome from those fairly undistinguished parents.
He is lean, without the jumpy Chihuahua traits. He
has a short, shiny coat, a loop tail, a haughty carriage,
and absolutely no grasp of his own insignificance.

As soon as I reach the hill that goes down to the
main road, both dogs stop with caution. They sniff
and settle upon the grass to wait for my return from
the mailbox. This is their boundary. I can't imagine
how they know it, but the property below the hill is
the frontage Mrs. Drummond told me she had sold
some years ago. Today curiosity conquered restraint
in the puppy. On my way back from the mailbox, I
saw that he had with extreme wariness crept halfway
down the hill. Suddenly he stopped and drew himself up. Behind one of the houses, a wirehaired terrier was watching him fixedly. The puppy hesitated,
but then, seeing that I was coming back, he faced
around and marched defiantly back to his boundary,
where he turned, pierced the terrier with an affronted
gaze, and barked with indignation until I reached
him. Mrs. Drummond calls him Junior, her "Hundred-Dollar Dog."

The dogs come to call at the cottage in the early
afternoon. Then I'm ready to take a break from the
typewriter and give them scraps. They do not like
the insides of houses, and wait outside politely. The
puppy, however, was intrigued today by the interesting things he suspected occurred beyond the door.   *63*

I invited him in. He balked, in a terrible state of conflict, spooked by the door itself. Flies swarmed past him, through the open screen. I shut it. He then stood with his front paws against the screen, peering in. I opened it again. At last, fast as a field mouse, he rushed past the perilous entry. His mother followed at once, fearful of missing anything.

My mother had come for the weekend, and she watched while I began to train the puppy to sit. He mastered the art of begging in five minutes. Rewarded with much congratulatory petting, he became unwilling to leave. I held the door open, but neither he nor his mother budged. They stared up at us worshipfully. Suddenly Mother said, "Why, she has only one eye!" It is true, but I had forgotten it. Mrs. Drummond had told me that Babe had torn out the other eye in a burr patch the year before. Her hair is so long and matted over her forehead that unless she throws her head back it's scarcely noticeable. Besides, I had grown used to it because the dog herself appears not to suffer from this physical defect.

My mother is very much drawn to Mother Babe, and watches the animal closely. "She's clumsy," she says, "but not because of the eye."

Mother has brought with her a large box of fall color, plush velvet sumac, hard teasel, and small orange berries of bittersweet that she gathered in the woods near her town. She is sorting them in the kitchen now, into smaller boxes which she will send to her sisters. Here's something different, something you can't find in your mossy Louisiana flatland, in your Kansas plains, or along your California shoreline. Her family is close and scattered.

I like to think of my aunts opening these boxes. Isn't it *like* her, they'll say, to tramp through the woods plucking up "something different," something wild? The gift may recall to them some remembrance of her as a child, when they all knew hills, woods, streams, and the country mornings that habits of city living have made exotic. She herself seems to remember as she sorts the stems, and so do I.

One Christmas morning I found in the living room a thorn tree four feet high. She had brought it from the Delta land and placed it there. Its bare branches, with a natural polish like silver, tapered slim to sharp, prickly ends. Its distorted shape and odd center of gravity delighted her. She decorated it with ribbons and tiny gifts. The thorn tree lived on long after the holidays, for like these dry flowers it seemed to tap the air for sustenance. Visitors remarked upon it with lifted eyebrows: "A thorn tree. How grotesque!" And yet, they would concede its unlikely aptness. "It suits you, though; it really does."

Feeling my own shortcomings sometimes makes me angry or cynical, and therefore at least partly blind. When that happens I should bear in mind my mother's thorn tree. She is a woman who has declined to grow hardened or dismayed by what she finds, but chooses instead to love the thing that makes her wonder, that stirs some differentness she feels within herself. What could ever destroy a woman who can embrace a thorn tree? Not the tree itself. Hers is not quite the nightingale's sacrifice: she asked no miracle flowering of it but merely adorned it herself, and survived. They led their separate lives, she and the tree in its own corner. I think that I am like her tree and that she could give me no better defense than it merited. "See this," she might say, "my only child, different and a little wild, perhaps grotesque; but festooned with ribbons and tiny gifts, she suits me. I can take pride in her. I have faith in her, whatever she is, whatever she means."

Today we watched as the Hundred-Dollar Dog took a bone for the first time. I placed a platter outside. He approached it, swiftly chose the largest bone, grasped it in his teeth, and ran with it to the nearest bush. It was so large that it dragged on the ground. The mother approached, and he growled her away ferociously, as if he had never seen her before. Then, later, she refused him her milk for the first time. He tried to nudge her over onto her side as usual, but she declined to be nudged. She bit his ear, his back, his tail, and shoved him away so firmly that at last he gave it up and trotted off in disgust.

A kitchen fit. Degrading. The immediate cause of such fits is usually the same: lumps in a sauce. The usual course the fit takes is that I bang a spoon against the pot, stamp the floor, and shriek. However, tonight there was a further consequence. When the spoon struck the stove, it also, with fiendish malignancy, pushed itself against the pot top and caused it to clang to the floor with a reverberating shock. Minutes later I realized that the puppy had deserted his begging post in the kitchen. We found him at last, cringing beneath the couch. I burst into tears, and Tom had to console us both. "It was an accident," he told us patiently. Useless. I felt utterly overwhelmed by a sense of hazard, a prey to chance. Most of the cruel things in life are accidents. . . .

And after a smooth-sauced dinner, domestic serenity restored, I pluck at the guitar. Why do I remember, of all songs, the cruelest lullabies? A bayou song: "Go to sleep . . . in the canebrake the crocodile waits for you. . . ." And another from these very hills: "Hushabye . . . down in the meadow, can you hear? cries the poor little lambie. The bees and the butterflies are plucking out its eyes. The poor thing cries out for his mammy. . . ." The slaves who invented those macabre lyrics set them to such tender melodies. . . . All life is cruel, and self-forgiving.

The time is going swiftly. In my trunk is a wraparound skirt I thought I could use, for it was too large. But it is several inches short of meeting now. My first euphoria was displaced by the contentment of the early fall. The days are shorter now, and another shift has taken place. I haven't slept tonight, but walked restlessly about, and cried. It is lovely outside. The pond is almost crystal in the moonlight. The fields stir with a light fall wind and occasional life. Tom sleeps soundly, with one foot, as always, uncovered. A peaceful calm pervades the house. What is this wild alarm I feel?

I felt proud of myself last night for not waking my husband. But this morning I could scarcely look at him. I am ashamed that I cannot feel happy.

Again, the same blank panic. Last night I walked like a ghost again. Then suddenly a phrase crossed my mind from Simone de Beauvoir. She tells us that the trouble with women is that the "species is gnawing at their vitals." That is an irresistible metaphor, and a sad denial of womanhood as well. And it occurred to me that there *is* a ghost in the house, of the old generation that was in terror of the abuses of the flesh, a Victorian ghost trying to get into my bones and gnaw at my vitals; not the species itself but the spirit of those wrongheaded servants of the much-maligned Queen.

I touched my husband's shoulder, and when he stirred I asked him to hold me close. The gnawing stopped.

Couvade. A modern couvade is becoming socially and medically sanctioned, as we find more doctors like my own admitting fathers to a delivery room. I think men are still queasy about it, though, and would prefer to stay out of this affair of begetting. They would rather not think too much about the strange thing that has placed their wives at a remove. Tom's great quality is that anything strange appeals so strongly to his imagination that he must find out everything he can about it. *His* couvade, he says, will probably last all nine months.

He has shown me a monograph by Allan Holmberg, about the Siriono in Bolivia, which describes a true couvade in which the husband is confined along with his wife to recover from the ordeal and to ensure his child's well-being. Those people do something to their newborn infant that I found very touching. They shape its head with their hands, molding it so that the child will be beautiful. The photographs suggest they may have some success, for the children are lovely. But what first made them unhappy with the nature of the race? What forest opened, or what sky, to show them some better ideal than they saw in one another, to convince them that man is born an imperfect creature in need of immediate improvement?

"Come on here into this house," said Mrs. Drummond. Today I used her sewing machine to make some crib sheets. She greeted me as usual but with a distracted look. Her television set was turned on, as was everyone's that day because of the latest international crisis. Her memory machine was also turned on.

Mrs. Drummond's memory machine behaves differently from others I have known. Possibly it was designed like others, as a buffer against the pain of truth. But Mrs. Drummond treats it more like an electronic brain. She programs into it every fact she

knows, hard or soft, every knock or shock her flesh
has inherited, all data she can lay her hands on. The
result is that instead of coming up with a punched
flat answer, the machine is vengeful, balks, digests
nothing, sifts out no pain, and merely spews back exactly what she has put in. It gives her no help, and
sometimes she will stare in disbelief at the pure mis-
chief of its refusal to censor.

"I say these things, and I know how they sound,"
she said with a short pause. "Dreadful. You're young.
You want your baby to live a long life. I pray the
waters will spare us all until he may be born, at least.
But I also pray with all my heart that it is over before
he comes to manhood and suffers what They are preparing us for."

The girl Dorrie was sitting slumped before the
television set, and didn't answer when I greeted her.
As Mrs. Drummond talked, Dorrie reached forward
and turned up the volume. She seemed to be paying
no attention to the screen, however, but shifted restlessly, glanced at the telephone, scratched her head
with a hairbrush. She had touched up her roots. The
insolence of her manner irritated me.

At the sewing machine, I was placed at the ter-
rifying advantage of simultaneously receiving the offi-
cial version of events from the television set on one
side and on the other Mrs. Drummond's version from
her memory machine. When I began to stitch my
crib sheets, I was thus taken up with three concur-
rent forces. But crooked hems have never bothered
me. What does is this: of the two convergent stories,

neither sounded less fantastic than the other, yet both had the deep reality of a dream.

On the television set we saw a world divided in half. The leaders of the one half were angry because of something the other leaders had done that they believed threatened the total security of both halves. If the demands of the angry leaders were not met, then the total security would no longer be merely under threat but doomed. Speeches were being made, not about the balance of power, but about the angry belief that missiles aimed at one side from a nearby island are more threatening than missiles aimed at the other side from a nearby border.

Mrs. Drummond's memory machine saw the world divided, too. And had a vision of immediate doom. "*At any moment!*" she cried with such ferocity that I looked over my shoulder.

"It's my second sight," she told me. "I was born with a veil, and have predicted many things. I predicted both my husbands' deaths, you know, by seeing a star fall. There was nothing to be done. I foresaw and was ready to bear the widow's weight. I'll bear it all my life. I foresee that too. Once upon a time, they might have burned me for a witch, but not now. And why? Because everybody believes, one way or another, the truth of what I see."

It is to happen at any moment, she repeated. Probably this very afternoon the warm sea of prophecy would begin to swell, slowly seeping inward over the hills to swallow up the faithless. It is as has been foretold. Radioactive fallout has been prophesied.

Fire first, then flood, then extinction for one thousand years. "The time to choose our side is now. Will we bear the Mark of the Lamb or of the Beast? For after our one thousand short years of grace, the Beasts must rise up again and be judged and everlastingly condemned. It will come as has been witnessed. Fire, flood, pestilence, destruction, death! The day is at hand."

"Balls," said Dorrie, letting her feet flop from the couch to the floor. But probably seeing I was of a mind to shake her, she turned down the television set as if to suggest her remark was meant for Mr. Khrushchev on the picture screen.

Mrs. Drummond accepted that interpretation. She said: "Let's have some peaches. I put up the best peaches last fall you ever tasted."

It is not surprising that Mrs. Drummond connects in her mind witchcraft and her religion of evil prophecy. The time to look for witches is when evil crops up. Burn the witch, and evil is reduced to ashes, too. Mrs. Drummond thinks she is safe from the basic fallacy of witchcraft today for a very interesting reason: her evil vision, one way or another, is shared by all. It is a fact that Mrs. Drummond's sect is gaining ground in these days of Instant Death. The world itself is a modern witches' caldron. Boil the warm seawater and stir in the pre-mixed lethal dose. We *expect* the world's end. And it is known that man's beliefs are defined by his expectations and that his rituals express the meanings of his hopes. Why not hope for a quick and early end, pledge ourselves to the Lamb, and prepare, once our dealings among the ungodly Beasts are ended, to enjoy the fruits of the kingdom? Thus we are, while among the Beasts, justified in how we treat with them. Fair play's the rule only after one thousand years, when we are separate from them. For that reason alone, why not subscribe to a prophecy of doom, not in fear but in the elation of commitment. What matter if the commitment is a drive to death? Why, this is no faith for the lunacy fringe, but a clear statement of the doctrines of the day. Let all join in and sing its ghastly truth!

While I ate the bowl of whole round peaches— the best indeed that I have ever tasted—Mrs. Drummond inspected my hemline. And the memory machine betrayed her with a burst of candor. "It's crooked. Never saw such a crooked hem." Then she laughed. "But don't you mind. You'd never notice it on a galloping horse."

I think Tom's couvade will take the shape of a "southern experience." Depression, my chief symptom, is not in his line, even in sympathy with me. But his exuberance is under stress. In his academic experience pettiness has not held its own for long over achievement. But here, because a handful of exceptional people have immediately accepted him, he is viewed with suspicion. There is not exactly a competitive spirit; it is more like an intellectual chain gang, in which many are linked by insecurity and whipped toward the goal of a more solid cult of mediocrity.

My method of ironic withdrawal from the pervasive genteel hypocrisy does not recommend itself to him. Nor can I in honesty recommend it myself, for its value is essentially negative.

We spent the weekend at my mother's. In her little town, men come to sit at the courthouse square, and their daily occupation is to whittle sticks. The sticks assume no shape, no design. At day's end, the ground about the square is littered with parings and the men are gone. Another folk custom that may be observed is a Sunday procession of cars at the square. The cars slowly revolve around the courthouse. As many are parked at the square as there are places for. The occupants watch the automotive promenade and exchange gazes with one another but little talk. In some other culture, Tom would take notes, slowly establish communication with a few informants, and gradually record the way of life. But these strange Americans fail to excite his scientific curiosity and have begun to fill him with annoyance and frustration. He sees them somewhat as I saw the women of Mexico, I think, wilfully revolving in a half-light, surrendering without a murmur the larger share of their human rights. He laughs, of course, and is more humorous than I about the things that bother him. But the general debility is like a backwater at floodtime: it seeps under even the threshold that is set upon strong stilts.

I felt the first stir of life today. Here in my little study, alone in the house, I sat still for a long time, both elated and disappointed. So that's it? Just a little scratch of tentacles? Margaret Mead tells us that in Bali they call the unborn a caterpillar. Outside my window, across the pond, the trees have been only a blur of brown and green. But today I saw a maple tree, completely red. It must have been turning for some time, but I hadn't noticed. It seemed to burst out, flaming in the sunlight.

For a girl, we hope for Tom's sister's fair, delicate skin, and Tom's own wavy hair, and my mother's small ears. A boy will be named just Thomas after his father: no middle name. A girl will present a difficult choice among several names. Schools must be coeducational and tough.

We sat at the kitchen table, taking up these potentialities like touchstones. Underneath the car seat, we have a small box of pebbles we brought from a beach near Monterey—agate, jade, and jasper—that we mean to have polished one day. Our thoughts tonight are like those stones, cool with solitary promise, warm with color, smooth with time's use. Everyone inherits such pebbles, unlike any other, to sort and weigh with love. It ended in a dispute. I prefer Tom's eyes, which are large and brown. He insists on mine. How absurd we are.

Anger. At best it makes me ridiculous, as with lumps in a sauce. But I don't get off so easily as a rule. I have known it to explode harmlessly, but also to harden into a knot of malice. And now this morning it has lashed back at me. The result has been a fit of guilty tears for half an hour. Billy Ned, the hired hand, has taken to coming down to the workshop behind our cottage. He uses an electric saw. I never hear him during the week because my study is on the opposite side of the house, and of course he doesn't work on Saturday. But for the last few Sundays he has waked us up with his electric saw.

This morning the roar began at eight in the morning, and was followed by a stretch of hammering. It stopped at last, and I thought Billy Ned had gone. Tom was only half awake. Perhaps that was what infuriated me the most. "How can you stand the *screech* of that saw!" I cried. He would willingly have gone back to sleep, but I persisted in reviling Billy Ned. We must *do* something! He was inconsiderate! It was unbearable! I stormed about the room. Then there came the quiet click of the wooden latch to the workshop door being fastened. Without a doubt Billy Ned had heard every word.

And then, less than fifteen minutes later, Tom went to answer a knock. He returned with two pale yellow roses in full bloom. "Mrs. Drummond," he said. I ran to the door and called after her. She had never walked as far as the cottage before because of her leg ailment. I held up the roses and thanked her lamely.

She said: "I just thought of you when I saw them outside my window this morning. I thought they'd cheer you up in case this might be one of those bad days. It's a hard time for you." And that was all. She walked back to the farmhouse.

Today I took her some German chocolate cake for my sins. She came to the door with a shotgun.

"You come on here into this house," she said, and I obeyed, with my criminal conscience. On her sewing machine lay a pistol. "Loaded," she said. And there followed an account of her superior marksmanship, which I did not for a moment doubt. I set the cake down on the deepfreeze and edged toward the door, but she was blocking my passage. Stories of mountain feudings whirled through my confused mind, and I was convinced that they flared up from just such sparks as I had thrown out yesterday. I said I had to be going, that I had a lot of housework to do. "Well, keep your door locked," she said. I told her I was sure that wasn't necessary, but my light laugh was nervous.

"You're the limit. You're not afraid of anything, are you? I never saw anyone like you. You're not even afraid of having that baby, and here I am, an old woman with one foot in the grave, scared out of my wits."

My confusion had reached panic stage. "About having a baby?"

Her threatening manner exploded into laughter. If I had been listening to the radio, it turned out, I'd have known that there'd been a break at the state prison that morning. It's the same prison where Mrs. 77

Drummond was once a missionary, and it isn't far from here. No names of the escaped inmates had been given out, but she was mortally afraid that one of the men might be looking for her protégée, Dorrie, and might even want to use Drummond's Park as a hideout.

Mrs. D. has a strong sense of drama, and yet such things do happen. While she was telling me all this, the telephone startled us both. She still held the shotgun pointed in my direction, and by the time she had set it aside, Dorrie had run down the stairs and snatched up the receiver first. Mrs. Drummond stood beside her during a short, covert exchange.

"It wasn't him?" she asked, and Dorrie let a flicker of contempt pass before she answered.

"I *told* you he doesn't even know where I am. But I'm going anyway. You don't have to worry any more." She ran upstairs before Mrs. Drummond could answer. I noticed that her arm was no longer bandaged, although the place where her "brand" had been was covered by her sleeve.

Mrs. Drummond followed me outside with more confidences. She was very agitated, for the man she thought might be looking for Dorrie is a convicted murderer. Furthermore, Dorrie has been seeing her parole officer socially, and it can come to no good, for he has a wife. Not long ago Dorrie came in with a bottle of shine in her purse from which Mrs. D. saw her drink. Nothing could have disturbed the old lady more than the devil's brew, and she told Dorrie she couldn't have it on the place. "I'm like a mother to that girl. I can't help it. With my own children grown up and moved off, I have to do something with the love the Lord gave me."

Drink had worked on Dorrie's conscience that night, and very late she had knocked on the old woman's door and waked her up. She wanted to confess her crime. Mrs. Drummond had never asked her why she was in prison, but now Dorrie spared her no detail. She had washed away the blood from the front seat of the car, scrubbed the windows, mopped the floor. It took all night. Pail after pail of water she brought to wash away the blood of her lover's deed. All during her confession, she kept her hand pressed upon her arm at the place where his name had been blazed.

"Ever since that night," Mrs. Drummond said, "she's hated me. She was feeling guilty, and I consoled her like a mother would, and now she hates me. Can you tell me why? I *think* it's because she let me see the worst that's in her. But that sounds too *mean*." She leaned close to me, and her face took on its wild, prophetic look. "Do you know a mother's life is a hell on earth? Do you know what you're in for, the misery you can expect? They love you, but you can't help know the worst that's in them, and so they hate you, too." She hugged me suddenly and turned back to the porch. From there she shouted after me, "German chocolate is my favorite cake!" And then: "Keep your door locked!"

Dorrie is gone. I saw her leave with two suitcases in the parole officer's car. Mrs. D. asked me to go to the supermarket with her, and told me all about it. **79**

She has obviously wasted a good many tears over Dorrie's soul. She has telephoned the prison, and learned that Dorrie's lover was not among the escaped convicts after all. And besides, they have been caught. She has not exhausted herself in grieving, however. She is full of plans. She is going to turn her house into a rest home for the aged. "Old bones are afraid of dying alone," she said. "We can all pile up together." Meanwhile, she is planning to spend January at Miami Beach.

Our new passion for conceiving names has extended to the puppy. The breed name derives easily from the two parent breeds and is "Pekhuahua." But the name that Mrs. Drummond gave him, Junior, doesn't seem right. He is not a chip off a block; he's neither Mexican nor Chinese, but one-of-a-kind, which is why he suits us. However, there is something faintly familiar in his arrogance. At last we identified it. He looks like a Flamenco guitarist we know, and so we have named him Niño. His full name is El Niño de Almadén, after another Flamenco artist and the California wine district as well. We had a visitor when the name struck us, a pretty southern faculty wife. She said, "Why don't you get a proper dog?" It sealed our fate. Tom said, "He'll be a first-rate animal." He jotted down for her a genetic chart showing the reproductive undertaking it would be to get another like him. She was unimpressed. He then offered a demonstration of the advantages of "hybrid vigor" over "inbreeding," which finally she began to see as an attack upon certain personal opinions of race she shares with other proper Southerners. That made her cut short her visit.

I have explained to Mrs. Drummond that Niño means Junior in Spanish, which by a stretch it well may. It also, of course, means "baby boy."

Now that it has turned cold, the dogs don't want to go out at night. We are in a state of conflict. We haven't yet paid Mrs. Drummond for the puppy, and so are doubtful about keeping him. Nevertheless, Tom has improvised a bed for him from my Mexican straw shopping bag. It is perfectly satisfactory. The puppy takes possession and will not go out. But there is Babe, the mother. She scratches fleas, which causes her elbow to thump the floor. And she makes an odd sucking grunt in her throat. She disgusts Tom. He puts her outside before we go to bed. But then I am awakened at four in the morning to her barking. She is just outside and has refused to go home, where she has a perfectly good basket in a warm place. I let her in. I warn her to stay in the kitchen where Tom won't be disturbed. But Niño is unwilling to share his bed, and growls when she draws near. The shopping bag is his own. He wants his own place now. She can go to the devil. She sinks on a pile of newspapers on the bottom shelf of the bookcase in our bedroom.

This has gone on for several nights, and yet her affections remain unchanged. When you approach, she wags. When you toss her a crumb, she wags. She makes me indignant. Why isn't she hurt by our cruelties? Tom declares that she is too stupid. However, he looks relieved when he finds that she has got inside.

Perhaps she *is* very stupid. She drags herself out of a thicket onto the yard, her fur trailing the ground, for all the world like a feather boa of a lady of easy virtue. She wants the burrs cut from her coat. I lay her on my lap, and even before I lift the scissors her throat rattles in relief. Mrs. Drummond says, "If she was to bleed to death, she'd get up again and drag herself through the burr patch." Stupid, maybe, but not simple. Sometimes she sulks. And then Mrs. Drummond says, "Ain't nothing the matter with Babe but meanness." You can see the malice in her. There is a flighty Chihuahua from Mrs. Drummond's, another female, whom she despises. Niño likes to leap upon them both in a feisty adolescent grasp of life. Let that bitch approach, cast a glance at Babe's son-companion-lover Niño, and her doll face is transformed. Antagonized, she bares the grin of some ancient Chinese demon, malignant and wonderful.

Two women are on the television screen tonight because they have taken thalidomide, a drug given for such tension as I have been having. Fortunately for me, it has been known for some months that the drug could do injury to the fetus. One of the two women has given birth to a child without arms. The other, the mother of four healthy children, has just returned from a flight to Sweden where she has had an abortion. The law in her state forbids abortion except to save the mother's life, and a county judge has ruled against a hearing of her case. In doing so, however, he has brought the law into question. The incident has raised some hard questions. The judiciary's comment dangles like a hot wire few care to touch.

We know that there are other peoples in the world who do not share our horror of killing an unborn or a newborn child. We know that in some modern nations such as Sweden and Japan abortion is looked upon as a contraceptive measure. We read of "primitives" to whom a deformed child is an aberration to be disposed of swiftly before it causes harm. But our own laws reflect our confusion. An unborn child does not qualify as a tax exemption. It is not, then, a dependent. *Is* it human? Certain theologies would not admit a dying infant to an afterlife without a ceremony of baptism, throwing its humanity into doubt even after birth. Yet these same theologies provide the doctrine against abortion that make our judge's wire so hot.

It is a well-known fact that abortion is widespread in our country and that illegality makes it the more dangerous and more expensive to the patient. Our laws against it are no more effective than liquor prohibition laws, and lead to similar abuses. The woman who chose to go to Sweden in defiance of local statutes had become such a *cause célèbre* as to

be outside the help of the local custom that would
have provided illegal abortion. On our statute books,
is she still a criminal, and is the crime, committed as
it was on foreign soil, exempt from the long arm of
our law? Probably she will be left alone, except as a
moral or immoral example. But that is where I do not
find her useful, for there is a troubling inconsistency
in her. Hers is an example of a disturbing quality in
our educated women: indifference to social problems
unless personally threatened, reluctance to take a firm
stand. She made an initial effort, but midway her conviction seemed to desert her.

Her first statement was a straightforward advo-
cacy of legalized abortion: she could not *in all conscience* give birth to a child whose chances were so
utterly hopeless. She spoke as an individual with a
certain faith in our process of justice, with a measure
of security that her reasonable demand would be met.
But her appeal denied, see what she says: "If I feel
this life stir within me, I will go out of my mind."
With what recklessness she abandons her argument!
Now she speaks with a dread of aberration that comes
straight from the tribe, and we see her making a
"feminine" retreat to "instinct," which is really trad-
ing on pity. She wishes to use all the illumination of
Western civilization to guide her, as she goes behind
the bush to throttle out in darkness the threat to her
sanity. Why did she abandon her own sense of justice
when confronted with its absence in the court? Let
her say, I have gone to Sweden because I believe that
it is *right*; then her sanity might glow with some in-

candescence beyond her personal concerns so that in time her judge's hot wire might be touched with the coolness of reason.

I suspect that before the ugliness of deformity menaced her family circle she never imagined extending her light outside it on so touchy a subject. Having four children and preparing for a fifth does not suggest the strongest social consciousness of our overcrowded world, at least in a woman not religiously persuaded against abortion.

As for the other woman on television tonight, there is nothing to be said. She held her baby up in her arms to expose its deformity to the camera. Growing from its shoulders were the flesh of hands that looked like the flippers of a sea lion.

Sometimes I think today's women are inclined to look upon the activities of the feminists as a silly stage in our development, like adolescence. And there was a certain absurdity to the movement, as there is to any effort pursued in dead earnest. But having passed through adolescence, many of us hesitate indefinitely at the threshold of maturity, unsure we like exchanging the liberty to be silly for some drudgery that may merely go down the drain. And so we do not make the most of our franchise, nor do we hasten with that clear-cut "woman's work" also begun in adolescence—birth control. It sounds like somebody else's problem, something Margaret Sanger thought up for the foreign multitude. We know that the greatest resistance to it stems from ignorance. How can it apply to us with all our university degrees? At the very most, we reason, it should serve those outcasts of the "welfare crowd," as Elvira contemptuously calls it. But what is to inspire them to forego what many have found to be a means of survival? If they look for an example among those of us who can *afford* to govern our own lives, they may look in vain. In fact, there is just a possibility that many of us may also, in our way, use childbearing as a means of survival rather than take on the possibly more difficult burden of governing our own lives. And the result is the creation of a dangerous domestic multitude, which Margaret Sanger and others also foresaw.

Can it be that we know these things and are afraid to act upon the dictates of our conscience? Is childbearing a vested interest that each of us clings to as if she were a corrupt politician? Most of us are not crusaders, and find it difficult to make a symbolic gesture. But we are stirred to our depths at the thought that our baby might not be healthy. Legalized abortion would be only a small step toward ensuring that the children who are born are healthy and wanted. But giant steps are needed not so much in the courts as in the conscience, where we must finally understand that a threat to "society's" health is a threat to our own.

Mrs. Hope and the Green Fairy. Yes, today's visit to the hospital was a page from a children's book, not from Grimm's tales but a modern pretty book. Ten mothers went to Mrs. Hope's "preparation" class, already prepared in their minds for something more fantastic than the bland fare that was offered.

Mrs. Hope brought out drawings and charts to illustrate the oft-told tale, and all the little mothers knew the text by heart. "Here is an egg. Here is where two cells unite."

Three student nurses were present. One of them told me that Mrs. Hope, a teacher at the nursing school, had worked for years to persuade the hospital of the usefulness of preparation classes. She is a graying woman with a generous, tactful smile. Her job is difficult. Ten pregnant women have been sent to her by as many obstetricians. My own doctor has told me that Mrs. Hope and her student nurses will teach me how to reduce the difficulty of labor through relaxation and breathing exercises. This, then, is the famous natural-childbirth process, but the term is assiduously avoided.

Mrs. Hope's way of getting started was to inquire of each of us what we expect of her. She went around our circle and spoke to each of us by our first name, a southern mannerism intended here to put us at our ease, as all of us are southern. Nevertheless, the expectant mothers either blurted or mumbled their answers. They have the poise of good educations, but this is an unfamiliar experience. They spoke of what they had read, what their doctors had told them, and of friends' accounts of childbirth. At last, Mrs. Hope came to the lanky brunette who sat next to me. She hesitated, and finally came out with the terrible truth that was in all our minds: "Well, pain makes me nervous," she said.

There was our common denominator: fright. But I soon became convinced that Mrs. Hope was searching for another one. All her nice charts and graphs would have been more suited to a high school hygiene course. Here, they produced the unreal atmosphere of a briefing session before combat. Pins on a map, chalk on the fingers, when a photograph by Mathew Brady, say, might better inform the mind. She at last established that all ten of us were there out of open-mindedness, that conditions might not prevail to favor delivery without sedation or anesthetic, that one of the ten might, according to statistics, have a Cesarean section, that circumstances would dictate our individual treatment when we had come to term.

She spoke a little of the changes that have occurred in a generation in obstetrical procedure, in a shift away from the asceptic caution that had separated mother and child in a hysteria of sterilization to more humane practices. "We still have far to go, but thank God women have forced these changes!" She spoke with fervor, and suddenly I saw what she was saying. *Women*, not doctors, had forced the changes. Why, Mrs. Hope was a genuine subversive. Here was what she was looking for—a way to "prepare" all of us without offending any one of the ten divergent medical views we represented. How can she expect to succeed? Any school that attempts to be governed by such a mean runs the sure danger of mediocrity.

A mimeographed sheet of exercises for breathing and relaxation was distributed, but it turned out we were not to try them today. Instead, we were to see a one-reel film of a modern mother going to the hospital to have a baby. It would have made us all feel silly about our fears if we had believed it. However, it was so thoroughly edited that we were not fooled. The mother's only sign of stress was almost imperceptible perspiration on her upper lip.

A consideration of Mrs. Hope's problem and the problem in the obstetricians' books I've read has sent me back to Montaigne. He said: "If the body find itself relieved by complaining, let it complain; if agitation pleases it, let it tumble and toss at its pleasure; if it thinks that the pain evaporates somewhat (as some physicians hold that it helps women in delivery) by crying out with greater violence, or if that distracts its torment, let it give full vent."

Have we more wisdom of the body now? Anesthetics were welcomed because they freed the body of knowledge of its torment, so that its agitation ceased. But how welcome to the doctor was the side benefit of silence? In all the modern methods Mrs. Hope is trying to reconcile, as in the film she showed us, silence is regarded as a desideratum. Silence through relaxation, through hypnosis, through conditioned reflex, and so on. Silence is undoubtedly more comfortable to the attendant, but maybe a body needs to release its vocal energy so as to make room for new stamina. What else is a battle cry?

I had been looking for Mrs. Hope's classroom when I saw the Green Fairy. The hospital is labyrinthine, many new wings having been added on to its basic box design. One is easily turned around. In searching for the classroom, I stumbled upon the modern circular wing where the confined mothers were. I did not, however, pass through, for my way was suddenly blocked by a tiny person. She was delicately poised on reedy legs, dressed in a green gown with a green cap over her hair. She lifted a flower-stalk finger and said: "Don't go in there. The babies are out." Her immense brown eyes held an uncanny excitement, and she looked at my condition with what I took to be pleased concern.

The babies are out. It seemed to mean something important, but *what?* Would I catch something from the babies, who, released and out, might be running wild? *Out?* It wasn't until she had redirected me to our classroom that I understood. *Out* of the nursery. Imperiled by the foreign menace—me! Babies, I thought. The girl's eyes were smiling not in concern for my health but for my hopes. *My* baby would someday be *out.* I pressed my hands against my side at that wonderful improbability. Really?

It is a fact that my reactions are slowed. Anyone else would have known what the nurse meant by "out." I am also tongue-tied, and cannot sustain conversations with coherence. More than once, Tom has said humorously, "I'm losing you to Mother Earth."

I'm in a soft, sensual drift, in which I pet the dogs, walk, make things with my hands, lampshades, curtains, Quiches Lorraines. Last night at a party I sat with a mother of a ten-month-old boy, and she, a former French teacher, had Flaubert on her mind. What she had to say I'm sure was interesting, but it was lost on me. I am a cork, visibly afloat, but below in the deep water is my control, the lead weight, and how cool it is to be tugged mindlessly downward by the nibbling flash of life. Suddenly Flaubert's admirer turned with a warm smile. "I wonder if you'd like to use some of my maternity dresses? I remember how tired I became of mine." She had seen that I was only half attending, and she remembered what it was like.

I have seen it many times, that look of remembrance. I go into a department store to try on a maternity undergarment, and the woman who fits me thinks back. It has been five years, but she remembers exactly how much weight she gained and how many sizes over her normal size she reached. It is not merely symptom-swapping. Many women have come to bring me infant dresses their babies outgrew. They've brought a basinette, an infant seat, an aluminum pot I mistook for a spaghetti cooker but which turned out to be a bottle sterilizer. We scarcely need to buy a thing. Women do this everywhere, I think. In Mexico I saw them on the streets, their *rebozos* folded about them like the wings of some great prehistoric bird, making offerings to the one whose *rebozo* bulged with the newborn or the nearly born. It is more than

91

an act of goodwill. It is a response to the scent of life and our possession of life, which has always caused us to gather beside the hammock, about the clearing, within a manger. Nothing is said of it, but surely women like this arrived in advance of the Magi.

The expectant grandmother. She is possibly more possessed by hope than we, despite her longer experience with its treachery. For childhood and motherhood are to be her lot again, from this third vantage point of generation. Three, a mystic number, is rounding out her life, to make it a charmed, a magic, circle.

Little caterpillar, our prophets would give us a hex against grandmothers: beware her old wives' tales, her post-Victorian hangover. But it was not ever thus. Nearly all humans admit grandparents to their genetic rights, and so do we, our prophets notwithstanding. Nowadays, they often raise their grandchildren, at least in part, when, say, the parents must finish school or somehow fall apart. Many grandmothers read what one in our family calls Dr. Spook. They know the score, if not in their bones, then in their hearts. And there is one thing about the new estate of their charmed circle our prophets do not commonly take into account: it must be given back to life, or it is finished. The Navajo understand this danger. If they make a rug, a sand painting, any design, they'll never quite complete it, on pain of death. They wouldn't close the circle up entirely, but would leave a space at the two rounded ends where the spirit may survive.

Our prophets' hex would close the space, but it seldom can withstand this circle's magic, which is as tenacious as life itself.

My mother has come, she said, to make herself a dress on Mrs. Drummond's machine. She has joined a club in her town and they are giving a party. "They have invited the *men!*" (Scandalized.) It has turned out that I have a dress she can wear that she has always admired. I have made her a present of it. And so she had nothing to sew, except what she really came for. To make some maternity clothes for me.

She is meticulous and slow, and won't make a stitch without my surveillance. That is because I always redesign "Simplicity" to something more complicated.

Tom did not come home until quite late last night. Not because he has what anthropologists call mother-in-law avoidance, but because he is working too hard. He is driving himself to thrust away the negative ambience in town that he feels might hem him in. Why can't he ignore it? My mother sees it differently. Although I said nothing to her of my worry, she defended him. "He's pushing himself to catch up. A year ago he didn't have a baby on the way. He didn't even have *you*." Nor I him. Does it mean we have taken on too much too fast? To love a single other being is a big stretch, and now my mother reminds me how much most people expand to take in, a full cycle, and all at once. My doctor tells me that breathlessness is a common symptom of pregnancy, but I believe it is not caused entirely by the physical pressure inside us.

Then, when Tom did come home, he was utterly exhausted. "Help me to slow down," he said. I was suddenly oppressed by the strain of being loved by them both. *Her* greatest weakness has always been to indulge me, her only child. And Tom's weakness for me is equally great. I know now that at least one reason he is driving himself is that I am slowly, slowly being pulled away from him. I can't *give*, to anything outside myself.

In Mrs. Hope's class none of the mothers quite understand the breathing and relaxation exercises, and only two of the meetings are given over to them. We lay on tidy pallets struggling with our tensions, and many were confused. No one was touched at a point of tension. Again, I felt the purpose was undermined by an excess of gentility and deference. Doctors don't care to touch patients at a point of tension either, I have noticed, although they will acknowledge its profound effect upon our physiology. Perhaps it is too deep for them. It is often a local source of diffuse pain, the knotted muscle, but don't touch it! Attack the headache indirectly with the prescription pad. And this tactile aversion is sometimes carried to such an extreme that the result is rather like setting a broken arm with the injection of a wonder drug.

There was an objection in the class to the term "contraction" as sounding too self-conscious a substitute for the traditional "pain." Other submissions were equally self-conscious: reflex, flash, throb, even "stroke" to suggest the involuntary advance of time. There are very few pleasant words to convey spontaneous impulses of the body. Most hint at anxious or distasteful overtones: spasm, convulsion, paroxysm. . . .

Someone asked Mrs. Hope to show her how to squat, as I was doing. It aroused a stir of interest, for it is not recommended on our exercise sheet. Mrs. Hope said that "some" thought the position put too much stress on certain pelvic muscles. "Some" doctors, no doubt. I couldn't help remarking that a vast number of children arrive in this world from just such a position, and Mrs. Hope rewarded me with a generous smile. She has assisted at such deliveries, when she worked in the cotton country on a welfare team teaching grannywomen how to boil their scissors. Some of the deliveries, she said, were remarkably uncomplicated.

Because my classmates soon lost interest in the novel idea of freeing themselves from tension without any means of locating the tension, the meeting quickly degenerated into a discussion of the reassurances that can be found in any handbook, about breastfeeding, bathing a baby, and so on. Someone mentioned, to my undoing, the fontanel and the elongated shape of a baby's head after its passage through the birth canal. Many friends have told me they found it difficult to speak to the point about anything during pregnancy, that they were often misunderstood. I thought that I was different.

Remembering the Siriono, who press the newborn head to mold it into a more beautiful shape, I told the story. I also spoke of the Maya's unhappy habit of beautifying their children's heads by flattening them with boards. A pall fell over the classroom. Those sitting cross-legged on their pallets shifted their position. Uncertain smiles flickered and died. Mrs. Hope cleared her throat. "It really isn't necessary," she said in a very reassuring tone, "and could be dangerous. The head assumes its natural shape by itself, you see."

There was no way at all to correct the impression I had made without seeming to protest too much, so I merely sank back down the years into my primitive squatting position, in silent communication with my little caterpillar.

People say the season is unusually bitter. Equipment for clearing the highways of snow is inadequate, and the roads are always icy this far out. There have been many subzero days now, and our house is poorly heated. Tom talks of moving into town, in case the baby should come before the winter ends. I don't want to go. I love the unbroken fields of snow, especially in the mornings, when the two dogs run out to sniff the shimmering sheet of white, two black disturbances kicking up silver spray. Finding the delights of the ground blindingly damaged, they return baffled to the kitchen warmth. Niño couldn't run free in town, and I couldn't use the *cilantro* that will grow here in the spring.

Last night the snowbound silence was broken by a noise that woke us. "A faucet dripping," Tom said. I got up to see. The puppy was instantly at my heels, watching, guarding. It is his way. The mother, Babe, never stirs on such occasions. She had retired in the room where my mother slept, but now lay on her usual kitchen pad. She is hard to rouse with the morning kitchen clang, or by the scent of frying bacon. She merely burrows deeper in her pad until the puppy leaps upon her and drags her up by the ear. Then she stretches a languorous neck, opens her one bleary eye, and surveys the chilly offering of the day. Often she will fall back and turn over, like some dissolute debutante from a 1930's film and go back to sleep.

It was a lovely night. Outside our bathroom window the moon sailed on the surface of the frozen pond in a high cold wind. The banks and meadows cast a radiance to the sky. The bathroom faucets were tight, however, all four of them. So were the kitchen faucets. I went back to bed, and the drip started up immediately. Tom threw the covers off and inspected the bathroom and kitchen himself. No drip. And yet, settled down again, we heard it inexorably resume. We pulled the blankets over our ears. Then I realized what it was. It struck Tom, too, at the same moment. He stomped indignantly to the kitchen. It was Babe. Snoring.

My mother appeared at her bedroom door and said: "I had to put her out of my room. Couldn't sleep. But I'll take her back." Tom shook the dog by the scruff of the neck. "She has a deviated septum,"

he told us. And to the dog he said, "Postnasal drip!"
She opened her bleary eye with humble resignation.
"Oh, let her be," I said. Tom looked from one
to the other of us. What could he do against such a
stronghold of mothers? He let her go. Released, her
faucet started up again at once.

A fall, in the middle of a busy street. Hands and
knees. The weight is hard to get used to. It doesn't
suit lightheartedness. For no reason, I felt like skip-
ping with bliss, and just the impulse was enough to
make me stumble. Then confusion and embarrassment made me get up too fast. There was a startling
jolt inside. But, never mind, it was only a kick of protest against a rude awakening, followed by a turn, another kick, and a subsiding toss. I brushed off my
hands, which were skinned, and my knees, which were
bruised, and reassured the man who had helped me to
my feet. Just clumsy, just a scratch. But I thought:
Don't you see? I'm too beautiful to be hurt by any
fall. Haven't you *noticed?* Perhaps that's why I fell—
everyone turned and *saw!* This is what the romantics
mean, perhaps, when they refer to "the most beautiful
time of a woman's life." They've noticed how we
sometimes feel.

It began as a giggly and girly occasion, the final
meeting of the mothers' class, because the fathers were
there, and also because everyone was more uncertain
than ever of what might actually happen when her
98   hour came. Two fathers failed to come, but they were

both pediatricians. Among the others were a salesman, a chemist, a musician, and an internist. The internist plans to be present at his wife's delivery. He need not have come either, for he knows the hospital well, and to tour it was the purpose of that last gathering. First, Mrs. Hope made a little speech that reassured us again of our extreme individual differences. By then I no longer doubted she was speaking of our doctors. Mrs. Hope's uncertainty of how the occasion of delivery would be met had spread a contagion through the class. She had failed to give us an adequate method for dealing with the crisis, and now that same inadequacy was communicated to the husbands, who had believed that there were definite ways in which they might assist their wives. They had come for counsel, but Mrs. Hope could suggest no more than a back rub during labor. As it happened, our tour showed us that the hospital cracked a whip over Mrs. Hope's pretty little individuals, and snapped them smartly into line.

We had to march down the hall to the oldest wing of the hospital, into another era. There a trio of young women, wearing masks and green robes, helped us all into identical garments. White cloth boots were fitted over our shoes, green paper caps over our heads, and gauze masks over our mouths. "What can it all mean?" I asked Tom. He punched me, and said, "It's an initiation rite, hush." The internist overheard, and grinned behind his mask. He said: "It's why we become doctors. You get to dress up." One of the nurses pointed to a swinging door, and explained the *real* reason. Beyond that door, everything was sterile. Now we had all touched the outside of our getup with our unclean hands. What consequence if someone's robe in turn should brush against some gleaming object? I didn't ask, though, too apprehensive to mention it.

The labor room had to be entered two by two, in initiate style, because it was too small to hold more. This was the place expectant fathers would be permitted to perform their back rub. But how? There were two beds and scarcely space for a single person to stand between them. Should two women arrive in labor at the same time, both beds would be occupied. The beds were narrow and enclosed with bars, like cribs or bins for the insane. We were warned against gripping the bars, for that would increase tension. Why, then, were they there? Perhaps to keep the mothers from rolling off the narrow beds? We were invited to imagine two diligent fathers standing in the narrow space between those two beds, offering moral support and back rubs while their two wives, relaxed and silent, did their damnedest to refrain from gripping the bars.

The delivery room took us further back in time than those Bedlam relics. It looked like an underground dungeon. There fathers are taboo, except for those with influence, like the internist and my husband. We were shown the delivery table, a narrow slab, to which the mother is transferred in the final stage of labor. And although Tom and the internist diverted themselves with redesigning the table so that it became a kind of flexible high chair that would accommodate the position a woman more naturally as-

sumes in giving birth, what we have to deal with was
before us. A flat leather-and-metal trap, with plates to
strap down legs and leather wrist thongs to hold down
hands. I have been unable to lie flat for some weeks,
but doubtless the equipment is effective.

Whatever the good intent of Mrs. Hope's fairy
tales, here was proof that she has been speaking to
some dream of the future and that her profession
still works with the implements of the past. No longer
giggly and girly, the initiates filed out, grimly refreshed
by truth.

Even with the baby's things on the top shelf of
the closet, where you put things you won't be needing
for a long time, we are beginning to believe in its existence. It is no longer some*thing* but some*one*. That
is because Tom can feel it now as it moves, when for
so long only I could. No longer a Balinese caterpiller
twisting in a tiny dance, it makes mammal shifts and
turns.

New York. When I lived in this monster city, my
life seemed quiet and reflective, as indeed it was, relatively. Out-of-town visitors geared it up, prompting
ritual visits to theater temples and feasting sacraments
that brought on the consequence of morning setbacks.
More often than not, the "pace" of New York life is
caused by those who come to visit and could not possibly live here. Now we have come for some holiday
fare, and invoke the myth of the pace. How is it possible that people can live at a never-ending party? *101*

If the visitor brings the party, or makes the occasion for it, there's something else that happens to him in New York. I think he sees what he brings here sometimes to the exclusion of what else exists. I have known some visitors who see nothing here but Puerto Ricans, Jews, and Negroes, others who see only celebrities. This time, perhaps for the first time, we see baby carriages and small dogs.

And also many pregnant women. Here, where I do know the Underground of other patients, I can ask my question: "Is natural childbirth a passing fad?" I find the partisans are as strong as ever, but I notice a discrepancy. They say their fear is reduced, that they do relax and "go with" the labor contractions, but that often at the final stage as the child is born they will accept sedation or an anesthetic. Now, that is the moment when a mother is supposed to feel that strong sense of achievement, when the difficulty of labor is at an end. Why then? The partisans say that sometimes they are too tired for the final push. It is as if my hunter, with his spear poised upon the pulsing heart of his prey, should decide at that moment to lie down and take a nap.

Something is wrong here, perhaps after all with the American women rather than with the doctors I have been holding responsible. We women lay claim to no-nonsense, and fear is nonsense; therefore we like a theory that disposes of it for us. But would we like our other emotions disposed of as well? I remember the girl I overheard in the doctor's office, who struck me as eager to be unconscious in order to avoid the rage childbearing made her feel. And here we have the other side of the coin. I believe these partisans, some of them, were unable to bear the thrust of success, the full power of joy. I asked about that.

"It takes a lot out of you," somebody said. And so the doctor, as wary as any American of the limitations of doctrine, comes to the rescue with his "adaptation" for the American woman, who doesn't know —or doesn't want to know—her own strength. Mrs. Hope was probably right to praise women for bringing about changes in practice, but she may also be right in saying that we have far to go.

This reprieve in the city has freed Tom from the southern "chain gang." We link arms on the chilly streets. A brisk wind turns a corner and leaves us in a stillness, and there bursts a phrase of Handel from a Village church: "For unto us a child is born . . ."

Mrs. Drummond telephoned our cottage this morning from the farmhouse. "Well, at least the telephone lines aren't down," she said. That is because last night there was no electricity for some hours. "Now, you listen here to something important," she said. "You've got to move to town. That's all there is to it. This is no place for a new baby, and that baby might come any minute." I told her that it wasn't due for some time, but my size convinces her it will be premature. "The pipes have burst. Look out your window and see what's what." Near the house Billy Ned and two Negroes were digging in the snow. "They've **103** got to dig up I don't know how many feet to find out where it's burst, and meanwhile we've got to haul water, even drinking water. It's a mess here, so you get on out."

It is undeniably a mess, and cold. But I want only to drift, drift.

Evolution cannot be finished with us. Consider the kangaroo. She carries her child inside her only briefly, and then brings him out to live in a pouch. This is true of the possum as well, and I am toying with the sophistry that as the oldest surviving species it may be richer in wisdom than our own. I should like to try the possum pouch for a few days.

Immobility has reached its nadir. And the bed size has shrunk. This morning when the alarm sounded I was turned away from it. The process of shifting my weight from one side to the other without falling out of bed is so elaborate that by the time I reached the clock, it had run down. This undertaking so exhausted me that I fell asleep again immediately. The result was that Tom overslept and will be driving too fast on icy roads to make his class.

I used to long for a child. I can remember those feelings. Some art critic or other has said of the paintings of Georgia O'Keeffe that they cry out "I want to have a baby." Those lean longings can have the powerful tension and ecstasy of art. They also have an immutability, like a dream, an ideal. But once the ideal gives place to an actual core of reality, our passion undergoes a subtle change. We do not feel creative, in anything like the sense of being captured by some brilliant light. And eventually the nagging of symptoms makes us all but forget the wish that has caused them. I endure the fundamental duplicity of the circumstance. What I have wanted is at hand, but it has little emotional resemblance to what I have imagined. Reality may not disprove a dream, but it can transform the dreamer.

Now I begin to think that those longings may have been entangled with elements imposed from outside my nature. From a very early age we women are told that we must bear children in order to fulfill ourselves. If we fail to do so, we cannot help but be overtaken somehow by a sense of inadequacy that must infect everything we do. Everyone wonders what is wrong with us. Why can we go so far, and no further? Is there, perhaps, after all, some natural weakness? I wonder if these questions cannot in part be explained by this imposed belief that we *must* breed and bear children in order to come to woman's estate.

My doctor has remarked that what matters is not how we bear our children but how we live with them. Yet that fear of inadequacy seems to persist even after our children are born. We live with them in dread of failure, and when they leave us we don't know what to do with our lives. I should like to imagine a healthy woman who had never heard in childhood that barrenness would blight her life, but I cannot. We find horrible examples among childless women to support this conviction: the ironic lady of letters, the driven female executive, the suicidal film goddess. But I wonder if instead our conviction did not itself create the horrible example. Call someone a witch long enough, and she may eventually beg to be burned.

Again, I am thinking of war together with childbirth. Let men go for a century in which no one believes "A man needs a war," and I wonder what might happen to this race of ours. And if women were left free to discover their own fulfillment, without having it fixated at a tender age, then I wonder if that "natural weakness" might not disappear. We shall bear children, always as long as the human race bears love. We cannot destroy biology—yet. But in our interpretations of it we can place ourselves at an unnecessary, even harmful, disadvantage.

I went up to see Mrs. Drummond and found she had another visitor, that miserable girl Dorrie. She has been married since she left here, and it is now clear she has been pregnant for some time. The parole officer is the father, Mrs. D. told me. Her husband is a young farmer from a town close by. Dorrie is trying to go straight. She brought a carload of winter vegetables she said her husband grew with organic fertilizer. Mrs. Drummond was overjoyed. But when Dorrie left, she turned grave. "A May baby, it's going to be," she said. "May babies are sickly, especially when they're a love child." I told her that I was a May baby and was physically pretty strong. But she remembered that my mother told her I had come of Cesarean section. "It counteracted your bad luck. You also are supposed to have the power to see spirits and find hidden treasure," she told me. Here was good news I wasn't aware of. Then perhaps I should welcome having my own baby born of a Cesarean operation, I said. But she flung up her hands—another counteraction. "Born! You don't call that a *birth*, do you?"

It is silly, but a goose walked over my grave. Was *I* born then? Do I live?

"They" are going to have a quarrel. Their first. "We" have talked about it, and think they are ridiculous. It is over money.

"Their" money has run out, and "we" feel degraded that "they" consider it worth fighting about. Of course, "we" do not like to think about money, and so "they" are really angry at "us."

It is said that money is a major cause of divorce in America. Can it be true? The money purse pulls its strings, from which we dangle like marionettes? Probably only among those who evade holding the strings themselves. But "we" are guilty of it. The strings are, after all, as long as the battle of the sexes and as entangling. They can tie you up in knots.

What prevents an early and reasonable foreshortening of these strings is that women historically have the upper hand of dependence. A string must be long to reach that hand, and she may hold on tight, letting it trip her husband up. She should be strong enough to help him to his feet, but never with the upper hand. She ought to forego the advantage of false femininity altogether, hold both strings at a level height while he cuts them down to equal size. The vanity of attaching   ***107*** money to male and female mores is then destroyed, and the two may sensibly decide the simple question: Which one is better at arithmetic?

The money quarrel has been averted by the expedient of a *deus ex machina*. A short story of mine has been sold. "They," thoughtless as ever, have gone off to Drummond's Park with wine and sandwiches to celebrate. But "we" have come home early to balance the books.

Woman's role. Ever since the need diminished for a clear division of labor in human activities, everybody has talked about it but nobody has done anything about it. That it differs from Man's role is undisputed, yet the creation story shows us no such clear distinction. It was Adam who longed for other human life and who rejoiced in its conception with one of the most maternal remarks of all time: "This is now bone of my bones, flesh of my flesh." And it was Eve whose discourse with the serpent upon the nature of wisdom led to our inheritance of the knowledge of good and evil.

It is said that the ancients who recorded the story were then emerging from a period of female dominance to a period in which they kept their women in low estate, but they cannot be held accountable that future generations built up a vast literature around Eve's "indiscretion." Those who describe her behavior as "eternal female" would point out that she placed

the blame on the serpent, woman-wise, not responsible for her own acts. And they might overlook Adam's classic self-defense: "The woman thou gavest to be with me, *she* gave me of the tree." It is bewildering to them that a woman should be a truth seeker, when she is clearly a childbearer. But I don't find a scrap of self-conscious femininity in Eve. She was a human being who wanted to know the score. She didn't like mysteries, and so she ate and took the consequence. She did try, like the only other living human, to weasel out of the blame for not having respected what in all reason we must consider God's caprice, but she had an inquiring mind, and nothing is recorded of her ever complaining that she learned what she learned.

Of course, such a view is not popular because it would take conflict away from the relations of the sexes and put it back where it started out, in heaven. Nobody gets a kick out of fighting with God. We prefer a scrap where we stand some chance, however slight, to win.

The clutch on the car has broken, and Tom must stay in town overnight with friends. He has telephoned several times to make sure that I am all right. It is not his fault. Nevertheless, I am bitterly depressed.

How is it for a man, in this period Tom calls his nine months' couvade? A point must come at which he loves his wife less before the end, when perhaps he will love her more. He sees her changed; he feels her changed; he suffers her physical withdrawal, surely not without some strong effect. Sometimes, not often, I

109

watch my man for a sign, with a coolness that baffles me, as if from a distant telescope where only a major change would show up, and I see nothing. At other times, equally infrequent, I feel a tender readiness to affirm our closeness that cancels out the fact of change in us both. But most of the time it is there.

I have heard of many husbands who leave their pregnant wives, but of not one pregnant woman who ever left her husbaand. Nature makes us more conservative at such a time and binds us to a nest. Even Dostoevski's idiot girl Lizaveta scaled a wall to lay her infant son upon Karamazov ground. We want our husbands more than ever during pregnancy, but not in a way very flattering to them. Hear the day's recital of complaint, give me your strength, and keep your manhood at a distance, please. His failure to react to such a ruling ought to give a woman some unease: perhaps she is married not to a man after all, but a saint.

Perhaps infidelity is a common experience for an expectant father. I don't know. The book that catalogs all those statistics is on the shelf, but it doesn't interest me. I know that to indulge in a wayward impulse would undermine his privacy, and he would not consider it. And then, there is the other privacy he does not want to violate, the private trust that our marriage is. Physical fidelity is implicit in it, but I don't doubt that its effect, at a time of increased dependence and simultaneous withdrawal, can be severe. I see a rattled sociability that is new, and a drive to work that is too exhausting, a mounting anger at the

110

"chain gang" that is too consuming. But perhaps I see these changes only from my own desire for calm, only in contrast to my own removed sluggishness. I can scarcely write one opinion when its opposite stands out against it like a bas relief, as something without which my argument is flawed. I am unequal to the desperate undertaking of setting down the truth. Bas relief: much as I want only to drift, I want also to know what is happening to us.

I have put a collar on the little dog, and he is shocked and affronted by it. He lies in the snowy garden on a patch of straw, in torment. The young reflexes are all there, a scent, a sound, a touch alerts him, but only for the moment before he remembers the offense around his throat. He chokes back his impulse to explore if he notices that I have seen it. He turns his head, proud and put upon, beyond the reach of tenderness.

That is how I am today. Beneath the level of tears, I shun the lift I know they could give me.

I asked the taxi driver if he had seen a wreck along the pike. An hour before I had been dreaming and was awakened by the sound of a crash. Was it part of my dream? I looked at the clock. Four in the afternoon. Earlier, I had tried to telephone Tom at his office, to ask him to bring home some medicine I need. Finding that he had already left annoyed me, and I had fallen into a sullen sleep. An hour later, the *111* hospital had telephoned to say that there had been an accident. They would tell me only that he was not critically injured.

The driver said, "I saw them tow off a car on my way here. Total wreck." Ours was green. Then perhaps there was a mistake, I thought. But I knew at the same time the mistake was the driver's. He pulled up near the worst curve on the pike, about a mile away from Drummond's Park, and pointed to a patch in the snow where oil had spread and where there was other clear evidence of a crash.

The ice had melted somewhat, and the road didn't look nearly so dangerous as before. On the shoulder lay a book of green stamps, a highway map, and a crushed wooden box. The driver pointed to the culvert at the bend in the road and said he thought the car had skidded and struck there. "That looks like part of a generator," he said, nodding toward a fragment of machinery. But I was looking at the box. Scattered about it were our pebbles—agate, jade, jasper—bright splotches on the snow.

And yet, all the way to the hospital, I could not associate myself with what had happened. All I felt was a disconnected graveness, as if I had heard bad news about a friend of a friend. And seeing Tom has brought about no change in this sinister state. I cannot understand it.

In his room in the emergency section, a nurse was putting his bloodied shirt into a paper sack. I noticed that first, before I saw him. He lay upon a

112

leather table, not a bed, for a surgeon had just left him. There were twenty-seven stitches taken behind his ear at the base of his skull. All he wore were Levis, and he looked like a small boy, dirty and barefoot. He saw me and spoke through a blur: "They called you at last. I was trying to go home to you afterward, but somebody stopped me and brought me here. . . . I didn't think I needed chains."

After that, he couldn't talk. I stood beside him and held his hand until he slept. What did he mean? He didn't think he needed chains. It sounded like a fragment of a dream. He was covered with bruises. His fingernails were lined with blood.

And now I am in the waiting room. I consider the event, and what he said. He had tried to walk the mile along the pike to come home, but someone stopped him. His head was cut open and bleeding. It's a lonely road. Sometimes you can walk for an hour and meet no one. A puzzled grayness has settled over me.

The practical tasks persuade me to move. I have telephoned about the insurance. I have telephoned my mother, too, to ask her to postpone a weekend trip. As I spoke to her, my voice shook, which was unaccountable, for I still felt nothing. *Your head rules your heart*, Angela had told me in Mexico, and I instantly denied it, choosing to believe myself head-strong only about matters of the heart.

In the waiting room, a ruddy-faced farmer has just learned that his eighteen-year-old son is being X-   ***113*** rayed following some other accident. He told me he couldn't reach any of his family. "I'll feel better when I can get some of my folks here with me," he said. I look at him, wondering. My own hard luck I've always begrudged anybody else. *Your head rules your heart.*

A doctor has just awakened Tom and taken his pulse. He is to be waked up every hour to make sure his sleep is not a coma. He looks at me, and his eyes are filmed. The doctor says he is still in shock. When the doctor leaves, Tom speaks without confusion, but he is very shaken. Now he has drifted to sleep again. "There're two of you," he said as he closed his eyes. He meant that he had double vision, and I followed the doctor outside to report it. He says that it will pass with the shock.

There're two of you. Where is the other one, the one that loves and feels?

Amniotic fluid protects the embryo from shock. Is there something like that protecting me? I continue to watch as he sleeps, and can make no progress toward him. My mind has mechanically adjusted to an inconvenience. Yes, now we shall move into town. In my mind, I have rented an apartment, dealt with movers, packed and unpacked. Elvira has even come to help. The most that has happened to me is that I seem willing to give up my immobility.

The fact is that I don't believe for an instant in *114* the possibility of his death. Such a thing is not a consideration of ours. Life is our concern. We have only begun to live as we wish to live, and what presents itself here is quite beside the point. Yet, if I try to imagine how he would behave if our positions were reversed, I know that it would be very different. . . . In his sleep he presses his hand to his forehead. They have given him nothing for pain, even when they took the stitches, because they are not sure how badly he has been injured. Am I asleep myself? It is like a dream, in which the dreamer moves without a spark of dread through the rubble of an earthquake, or cheerfully consorts with demons. I've had such dreams, and others too, in which some commonplace, a joke, a smile, a flight of sparrows, can thrust the weight of the sky against the mind.

Tom awoke briefly and reached for my hand. He still saw two of me. He smiled weakly and said, "I'm carrying the couvade too far." We joked about it, but he is deeply troubled that the baby may come now while he is helpless.

Today he is better. He will be moved from the emergency room for further observation and tests that may take a week. In the waiting room, the man in work clothes I saw yesterday was no longer alone. Several female relatives sat talking to him in muted, fearful tones. His son has to have major surgery.

My mother appeared at the door. Her head rules *her* heart, too, in its way. She had thought that I will need a car, and brought me hers. The man looked up as we passed him and gave me a pinched smile. "Some of your kinfolk come," he said. "That's good."

This last night in the country, I haven't slept. The insomnia had a vacancy at first. The night stared back with hollow eyes, dark and dispassionate. The baby moved, but not so much like a living thing as like a rock thumped in a gentle tide. A noncommittal calm pervaded the room. Even the sound of the sleeping dogs was not animal sound, but a mark of time. I might have been a dark shoreline before the break of life.

Then the rain began. At the first spatter of drops on the tin roof, I thought: The rain will wash away the rest of the ice from the roads. And then the events leading up to the accident itself lined up in the dark. I needed medicine; Tom could not be reached; I was annoyed. And then the accident itself. The car went into a skid, struck a culvert, and turned over. And it skidded—now I understood—because he had not thought he needed chains. If I had puzzled over that phrase of his, I had nevertheless reacted to it. When we seek the cause for any accident, what are we really looking for? I think I know. The blame. Blame fixes responsibility outside ourselves. How familiar is the sight of the inspection team, probing the debris of this air crash, that hotel fire, to no avail. Nobody is to blame. It makes us feel worse. And now I know that in the hospital it was no amnionic fluid keeping

out the bright color of relief, but a gray blanket of

blame. It was something I did not want to think myself capable of feeling.

The rain is washing away the ice. Tomorrow I must go to search for our pebbles, our touchstones, if the rain has left them there beside the road. But now I listen, as it strikes the tin roof with the hardness of hail or the hardness of truth.

My mother has tried to buy Babe from Mrs. Drummond, but the old lady will not hear of it. She said: "Why, I'll never forget the morning Billy Ned came into the house when that Hundred-Dollar Dog was born. Billy Ned said, 'Let me show you something,' and uncupped his hand and showed me a little ball of fur not much bigger than a hickory nut, and Babe was leaping and clawing Billy Ned's legs like a mother tiger. It's bad enough as it is to separate those two, but I couldn't get along without old one-eyed Babe." What we took for indifference, then, when she let Babe live with us, was Christian charity.

The moving truck has taken out the boxes, and I am sitting with my black notebook, waiting for Mrs. Drummond. Because my mother has gone home now, Mrs. Drummond has offered to take me and Niño into town as soon as she gets back from some errand of her own.

And now Babe confronts me with a thumping tail and an inquiring eye. I have just carried her basket up to the farmhouse and left it there. She sniffed it and immediately followed me back down to the cot- **117** tage. She has noticed that Niño's basket remains in the kitchen, but it is upright now and may not be sat upon. They both stood at my feet for a while, looking up as if some explanation might be forthcoming. The emptiness of the house disturbed them. They turned their noses from it and begged to be let out. They have gone out now for a final romp. In the hospital yesterday we talked of bringing Niño back often to run in the fields with Babe, but we know that probably we shall not. She comes back from time to time to look at me through the screen. Can she be searching her tiny memory? This has happened before, whenever a tenant has moved. Does she not know that in the human camp she can expect to be betrayed again and again?

Elvira has come again to help me get settled in the new apartment. Since she saw me last, she said, she had been wondering about something. "Do they really have Indians in Mexico? People who eat dirt?" I was up against a pedagogical problem, I saw: how to impart a little of what we know without distorting the whole. There are only a few starch-eaters here, I reminded her, and only a few clay-eaters there. And, like a coward, I diverted her with a question that had been on *my* mind since I saw *her* last. What had she meant when she said that violence wasn't always bad?

She thought a while, then gave me a golden smile. "It was about Katie. You know, I told you I took her kid home when I caught her feeding it the starch? Well ... I had to hit her to get him away from her." The baby has recovered, which proves conclusively for Elvira that the end justifies the means.

I asked her how her plans for moving away were shaping up. She looked uneasy at first, then decided to take me into her confidence. "I got a man here wants to marry me," she said. "Not a drinker. And he's good to my kids, so I think ... okay." She was very grave, and there was clearly something weighty on her mind. I wished her well with corresponding gravity. She said: "I got to ask you something. A favor. I been thinking about this marrying again, and I think women have got to be in charge, you know what I mean? My mama said that once, and I thought she was wrong. I didn't listen to her. But I been thinking about it a lot. You can't count on a man. You want to, but things crop up. They go off. It's wrong maybe to be all the time suspicious, but this time I want to get some birth control. I never had any, but this time, well—I've had enough trouble."

Thus Elvira, seeking to reconcile herself to the matriarchy in which she lives. In all the moral uncertainty she had outlined, there was at least one blessed fact I could assure her of as I wrote down what she needed to know: Women "have got to be in charge" of contraception if it's going to work.

Just before she left, she looked at me appraisingly. "You know, if you put it on in your hips, you going to have a boy," she said. "If you put it on in your face, you going to have a girl. But you put it on everywhere. I think you going to have twins!"

Boone Wrecks Another One. The sign is nailed
to trees all over this neighborhood. *Boone* stands out
in red translucent letters that glitter in the lamplight.
Beside the name is a sketch of a coonskin cap. Some
descendant of the frontiersman come to wreck another—what? Bewildering. Daniel Boone was never
known for wreckage that I know of. As I walk the few
blocks from our new apartment to the hospital, the
signs loom large against the oldest trees.

The tests have all turned out favorably, and Tom
is in high spirits. I told him I had retrieved our pebbles, and he looked at me with such love that when
I remember it now I want to cry.

Bulldozer and crane have solved the mystery of
Boone this morning. His men were at work, tearing
down a large gray stone house at the corner. There are
no Doric columns in this neighborhood. It is too old
for them, having been built before the Parthenon
craze. The dog and I watched for a time, he mourning
on his leash for his lost way of life. He slumped down
on the sidewalk and lifted a dour gaze at the fantastic
activity across the street. Humans are obviously not
sane, and he would cheerfully be shut of them if only
he knew how. The giant arm of the crane had flat-
tened all but the housefront, a façade of stone fastened to a wood frame. The arm crashed against the
stone façade, and it gave like pasteboard. The house
front swung away from the front-door arch, a panel
of twenty feet of stone, and hung in weighty balance

120

for a few seconds before it swayed backward into the pit that had once been the cellar of the house. It crumbled when it fell, and then the teeth of the dredging bucket seized and lifted chunks of it, separating stone from timber that was being burned.

I tugged the leash. As we moved on, I pondered the meaning of what was happening. We had come to live in the heart of Boone's territory, dying America itself. This neighborhood, built as a pretentious embellishment to the nearby university, had to go. Two blocks away, many Negro families have moved into the houses of this period that are not condemned as yet. And four blocks beyond, there lies the Hard Core, as sociologists call Elvira's neighborhood. But all along our block, the houses stare out hollow-eyed, their ugliness doomed. Our apartment house has already taken up the sites of two such houses, and the parking lot across the street has superseded three of them, for the three sets of cracked stone steps that lead from the sidewalk up to the lot are surely relics left by Boone's demolition crew. There are holes in the ground where the very trees on which Boone had hung his signs must have been uprooted. I think that I have never seen a clearer demonstration of how one ugliness is replaced by another.

Our next-door neighbor, Mrs. Harris, is a holdout against the dubious Boone, and she has her reasons. Eight of them are children. But there are other, shrewder reasons that she told me about on first acquaintance, with the candor people here enjoy. That candor concerns facts only: of religious affiliation, of *121* financial and social status. Gentility masks opinion, particularly about the Problem, or anything else thought to be controversial. Mrs. Harris spoke freely, not knowing that I can find controversy even in the air we breathe—which is smoggy. She was burning trash in the backyard of her gray stone house, as many large families here do, for garbage collection is a private enterprise, and expensive.

She has a slender girlishness, a wrecked fragility in her face, and wide, vulnerable eyes of green. She said, "Oh, yes, we sold our other house, that one there." She pointed to a white clapboard shell grown about with weeds in the block behind us. There, a pizza palace has been built against one side of the house, and on the other, a recording company's stucco studio wedges it in. She believes that the Boonedogglers will replace the house with a laundromat. The visual chaos already staggers the imagination. Behind the future laundromat two new apartment buildings rise, of bright orange brick. Mrs. Harris gazed off toward the dead concrete center of town a mile away, from where the smog was drifting. Twenty years ago, she said, this was a little country lane. Her husband grew up in the clapboard house, and used to raise beans where the record company stands. But when the block was zoned for commerce, Mr. Harris took the price "they" (anonymous "they") offered and bought their present house. And although this block, too, has a commercial zoning now, the Harrises plan to hang on until the price improves because they "need the space."

Citizen arrest in any form is rare, with its danger of involvement, and citizen arrest of urban blight must be rarer still. Complicated payoffs that extend even down to those most immediately effected would discourage it. Mrs. Harris laments the loss of the bean patch less than she enjoys the profit it brought. And thus our dying America is hastily reconstructed. Hundreds of new modern communities are thrust upon us in this way, like those fruits or vegetables that are pushed onto the market without time enough upon the vine. Sometimes they are impressively glossy and colorful but inside they may be pulpy, without nutritive value, devoid of the taste of maturity.

This afternoon Mrs. Harris stopped at my kitchen door, wearing a navy-blue uniform and the pert cap of the "Mothers' Patrol." She goes to a nearby corner every morning and afternoon to direct drivers on their way to and from a public school. "How do you have time for that?" I asked, thinking it was volunteer work. She said: "Oh, it's just for a few hours a day, and they pay us a hundred eighty a month, you see. That buys a lot of beans." Mr. Harris drives a delivery truck, and I notice that when she is away he manages to drop by to look in on the children.

Some lichens I brought from the country are suddenly thriving in the dampness outside the door. I found them in the woods last fall, attached to some loose bits of bark. I thought the winter freeze had killed them, but now they have crept to the surface of *123* the wet wood, faint orange stalks soft as wax on one piece of bark, and on the other, a dry green bristle. Their revival gave me a surge of hope. I noticed it this morning on my way to the hospital. There I found Tom dressed, released, ready to come home. The doctor says he must have a few days of complete rest, but his energies won't permit it. He is already pushing himself as hard as ever, after only half a day. The bandage is removed. The scar lies in a lucky place, just at the hairline, scarcely noticeable.

Now I see my doctor every week. His lectures still give me a lift, but even so I often come away under a cloud, foggy and unsure, like a good C student. I think I'll pass this elective, but sometimes I wonder if I shouldn't have chosen to sleep through the course. I'd still come out with a plus, even though the Rolls-Royce baby now seems as far beyond my reach as a Rolls-Royce itself.

Some of the terms are delightful. *Lightening,* the shift of the infant head into place for its push for life, transforms the heavy weight into a feather drifting down to settle on a gay canal. And *crowning,* the appearance of the dome of the head, trumpets a note of princely triumph. Even *labor* has a certain somber dignity. But other terms are not poetic. *Breech,* for instance.

"There," he said. "You can feel the head. It's in a reverse position." Why do I feel that *he* has put it there? He doesn't favor breech deliveries because of the danger of suffocation, except when there is what 124 he loftily calls a *bucket pelvis.*

Last night the baby's head took a downward dive, and I felt a kick in the ribs. But in an hour or two it had drifted up again to float on top of the pool.

I walk slowly, slowly now. But I walk. "You *walk*," cries a letter from the Underground. "O Pioneer! I did not budge. I laughed at the books that talked of lightening. I laughed at glorious natural childbirth. I laughed as the tears rolled down my cheeks." On the campus I can let Niño off his leash while I sit in vegetative numbness, insipid as a parsnip. I have no wish to stir, only to submit to the uses of nature. But Niño, running impudently across the blighted grass, demands attention. Some rancid morsel gripped between his teeth, he races past so that I may see it before he begins to devour it. I waddle to snatch it from him, and something gives in my right hip as I stoop down. Now every step is stupid with pain.

An hour of crisis at the Harris house. Niño and I were out watching Boone's men when two of the Harris children ran past us in tears and thumped at a neighbor's door. A fire truck passed, rounded the corner, and drew up in front of the Harris house. In a few seconds, a swell of smoke billowed from one of the upstairs windows.

The other Harris children were dancing in the front yard. Mrs. Harris was just beyond the door, telephoning her husband. Stumbling over the snake of a fire hose in the doorway, she came outside, followed shortly by the firemen. They were already gathering **125** up their equipment. One of the firemen told Mrs. Harris that they had discovered a short in a wire, but no fire had broken out. The fire truck was gone as briskly as it had come.

I offered to help Mrs. Harris open the windows to air the house out, and tied Niño to the tree in the yard. And that is how I happened to go inside her gray stone shell.

She left me to raise the downstairs windows while she and her oldest daughter, laughing in relief, went to open those on the other two floors.

A dizziness overcame me, not caused by smoke. It was the sensation of propulsion. I was in my Mexican time machine again. I hadn't seen a house so furnished since my childhood, for I have led a sheltered city life (and Mrs. Drummond's house, of course, was a museum of modern ingenuities). This old mansion has been converted by the Harris family into a kind of country house. The floors were bare, and there was little furniture. Panels that slide into the walls to create an arch separate the living room from the dining room, and they are locked open. The dining room is the parents' bedroom, and a brass bed sagged beneath a crystal chandelier, probably fixed there when the house was built. Beside the window stood a baby's crib. Beyond the swinging door to the kitchen, a long table was spread with an oilcloth cover.

I opened all the windows, wondering why the house oppressed me so. Not because of the poor
means its barrenness suggested, for there was no sign

of real want such as I might find a few blocks away among the starch-eaters. The smoke drifted out, but a static gloom hung about the room. I could see that there is seldom any light admitted to the house, for on one side our own apartment building blocks the morning sun. In a moment, the other children crossed the threshold into this half-light. The smallest boy clambered up the dark staircase calling in a timid voice, "Mama, is the fire gone?" Through the bright patch of a window, I saw Mr. Harris leave his delivery truck, and in a moment the whole family was reunited in the living room.

"Those damned wires," said Mr. Harris bitterly. "They're rotten." Mr. Harris has a lean body that is separated from his head by a neck so long and taut I had the lunatic idea he may have often hung himself from it. His eyes glitter with desperation. "Rotten. This whole place." He looked to the ceiling and into the corners of the room as if for further proof, so whipped that he could not meet anybody's gaze.

Mrs. Harris tried to ease his pain. "The fire truck got here so fast, Jim. They were just wonderful."

He flung up his hands in a wild, reckless gesture and spoke with fierce resentment. "And wouldn't they come just as fast if we were in the country? Every little tank town, every subdivision even, has its fire truck." His hands fell limply and he stared about with hunted eyes. "You just can't get away from them."

Something terrible and strange was going on in Mr. Harris, and if his wife had not been aware of it, or if a neighbor had not been present, he might have groped his way closer to the cruel fact of his predicament.

But when his wife said: "Oh, Jim, you don't know what you're saying. I couldn't drag you to the country," he shook his head and went upstairs to examine the burnt-out wire.

You just can't get away from them. What did he mean? Mrs. Harris knew her husband didn't want his old bean patch back, or even a rural patch of green outside the city. No, this accident had struck Mr. Harris in a place where he deeply wishes for a world that's free of fire trucks. What is a fire truck? A benefit, indeed, a bare necessity. Why, as he said, every little tank town has one. A fire truck preserves the structure. It saves precious lives and property. Yet somehow, in a corner of his private hell, Mr. Harris would sooner burn.

The children had begun to chatter, elated by the false alarm, and vaguely disappointed, too. Mr. Harris came back downstairs almost at once and jerked open the door of a closet. Looking for a wrench, he said. Suddenly he turned, and in a voice of even greater vehemence he said: "You kids get out of here. You make me crazy."

It was time for me to leave. On Mrs. Harris' face was a look of pain I wasn't meant to see. I went out with the children. There was really no place for them to go. The front yard is smaller than the living room, and the parking lot across the street is jammed with cars until late afternoon, when they sometimes play ball there. I took Niño from the tree I had tied him to when I went inside. Two of the children trailed after me, a little boy and his smaller sister. She is as beautiful and bright as he is coarse and dull. They think of me as a contemporary because I play with a dog. And sometimes with them.

The little girl has yellow hair and a tenacious smile. She told me about their dogs. They didn't tie them to a rope, she said. One-two-three-four-five, and all had got runned over. One-two-three-four-five. There was no place to go.

And I thought of Mr. Harris, and knew it was the children he just couldn't get away from. If a man is hard beset by children, he well might harbor some perverse question, secret even from himself: Is it not better after all to burn than to marry? The fire truck had saved for him all the treasure of his life. But perhaps there crossed his trapped mind an image of what he and the fragile girl he married had expected of life's variety before they were overtaken by an excess of life itself. Before they reached that point of balance where a blessing can become a curse. But seeing the madness that lay in such a thought, he deflected the torment and turned savagely to repair a rotten wire.

There is no place for him to go either. That is the terrible truth of his hollow house. There is no place in our world for a family of that size to exist.

Mr. Harris loves his family, and to preserve that love he keeps his hell to himself. He cannot say, "I'm all used up because of you," not even as a warning. Eight times eight is sixty-four. If each of the Harris children bows to an already enfeebled dogma and bears an excess of riches like their parents, there'll be the Devil to pay. Sixty-four grandchildren, Mr. Harris. I wonder if he's thought of that. The Devil surely has, and in his reckoning must see the infernal orange glow this city casts off at night as only a modest beginning, and the flash of hellfire in Mr. Harris' soul the merest spark.

Mrs. Drummond, should you look into the sky or your television set for your apocalypse, or into a neighbor's heart? What else can the legion do eventually but run like a swarm of lemmings, scrambling and scrawling over its own massed limbs, to tumble into the poisoned sea?

The ninth month. Such is my vision of family life in the ninth month. Little, come out and let me love you.

A retentive memory is an attribute I greatly admire, lacking one myself. I think that is why I keep this journal. I want to remember all this, even the worst. Yet memory failure is a blessing to some people, who tell me I'll "forget this last month right away." Or who say, "I don't remember having any trouble the whole nine months." Undoubtedly, subsequent events will work upon a memory to change it for the better.

And certainly I shouldn't like the memory of this last month to dominate my life. From day to day, the sense persists of being in a process that is going to run its course as if I weren't here myself at all. My own work has stopped these last few weeks. I feel no sense of excitement, no anticipation of what is surely going to happen soon. Just a strong impatience with the present: I am captive. There is nothing to be done.

Now I suddenly remember feeling this way once before. It was in Mexico, not twenty-four hours after I met Tom among a group of anthropologists working there. I went with them that day to see an Indian village, one of the poorest in the country. The people might have been in eternal mourning, for everyone wore black tunics with white pinstripes. Lacking the scientific objectivity of my companions, I saw the place as a settlement of convicts, and was ready to leave before the others had finished taking pictures. Tom walked with me up the hill outside the village to wait for the jeep, and a little boy tagged after us. No more than six or seven, he had a cache of cigarettes in his tunic, and he smoked constantly, holding the cigarettes in dainty, nicotine-stained fingers.

Suddenly the boy sprang up and said, "Here, I'll show you my father." Just beyond us in a hollow we hadn't noticed was a graveyard. The boy leaped down and placed his small bare foot upon a mound of freshly turned earth. His expression was noncommittal, and a curl of smoke drifted from between his childish lips. He turned to other graves, naming for us the relatives they contained, a sister, an uncle . . . death was a commonplace of his life.

After that, Tom began to talk about the people of the village. He told me something of their family *131*

structure and other things my memory has been unwilling to retain. The boy sat nearby, listening to our
unintelligible English words and gazing down on the
place where he would live out his short span of days.
I don't remember when Tom's talk shifted from the
Indians to himself. But soon he became excited, auto-
biographical, personal. At one point, he jumped up
and stamped the ground. The details of what he said
about himself have not stayed with me either, but I
remember well his abrupt, almost insistent enthusi-
asm. And I wondered, Why is he doing this? Then I
felt an inexplicable impatience: I am captive. There
is nothing to be done.

Perhaps on some level of the mind a warning
twinge is always felt just before our lives take a sharp
turn. The next day I was in love with him, and that
changed everything.

The X-ray department is very small, and on Mon-
day morning very busy. I listened while my doctor
gave instructions to the technician. He wants the doctor in charge to examine the first picture before de-
termining if a second picture is to be made. If the
infant lies in a breech position, then there is no need
for a second picture. I was led into a cubicle and told
to put on a hospital gown and to wait there for my
turn. The cubicle was so tiny that I had to leave the
door open to make the change, and I could not fail
to observe the others being X-rayed. A little girl sub-
132 mitted her broken leg to the light. An old man in a

bathrobe shuffled about looking for his slippers. I saw a pair at my feet and thought he must have used the cubicle before me. It was impossible for me to stoop down in that space, so I backed against the wall to let him grope for them. He lost his balance and fell against me. He complained crossly that he had had no solid food for a week, by way of apology. Then my turn came. Inhale, exhale. Take another deep breath, hold it. Then wait again, in the cubicle, while the picture is examined. "That's all," the technician came to say. "They found what the doctor wanted in this one." What the doctor wanted.

Tom is very distressed. This was the manner of *his* birth, and he feels a goose has walked over *his* grave. I am, he says foolishly, trapped by his genetics.

A long, cruel dream. I was obliged to back my car up the length of a block that seems interminable, in order to fit it into a parking space, the only space available. My backing is clumsy, and traffic swarms about me, going heedless upon its affairs. A fire truck clangs past me on the right-hand side, for I have swerved left as I backed. An ambulance and police car are obliged to pass on the wrong side, too. No one reproaches me or seems to notice my ineptness, but I am frantic with frustration and shame, even as I approach the parking space. I cut the wheel too late, and must try again, and as I pull forward to level off once more, I am awakened by the alarm.

133

Consultation day. I do not like the consultant, but to be fair I doubt if I would like anyone now. He is a subtle version of the first doctor I saw here. His pale blue eyes are like skimmed milk. He is deferential about my doctor's deference to me, but it is obvious that he thinks the consultation is unnecessary except to prepare me for the possibility that he may be the person who, in my doctor's absence, will make the delivery. Although he did not say so in so many words, he clearly believes that a Cesarean section is necessary.

After he had gone, my doctor slowly led up to the consultant's diagnosis, neither confirming nor denying it himself. I was having another of my delayed reactions, for only as he began to talk did I feel the disappointment Tom expressed last week, when the X ray was taken. The doctor talked a great deal, as if to give my disappointment time to run full cycle and subside. He even tried teasing me a little. I am unusually uncomplicated. Blood pressure, weight, better than average. "A most uninteresting case," he said with a smile. No troublesome sign in all this dense thicket of syndrome, he said, good-humoredly avoiding the state of my soul. Readers of sign are trained to the leaf, the tree, the pathway, and take little note of the forest itself.

He turned on a light behind the celluloid that I might see, marked off in centimeters, the inflexible shortcomings of bone. The spine slants where it should curve. He said, "In a normal presentation, we might not be concerned, but in a breech..." His words stacked one upon another, tidy notes from a lecture, and then a sentence: "If this position persists, of course, there is to be no crowning. . . ." No crowning! No trumpet blast? No regal victory? No triumph of achievement?

Defeat deflects back from the glassy rounds of his bifocals, and he continues to explain and explain. I might still choose to wait, for lightening may occur in labor, and lightening will be followed by crowning as the night the day. The choice is academic, for the chance of a shift in position during labor is very slight, but the choice to wait is mine. I must talk to my husband and then decide. The decision is as good as made. I glare at his bifocals.

Little, our noble scientist has turned into an academic grind before our very eyes. Never mind his tact and obvious concern. Never mind. He has said it: there is to be no crowning. The world shifts, wobbles on its axis, and turns upside down.

Scarcely anything goes according to plan. We know this—everyone knows it—but we continue to make plans and to believe in their probability. The irrepressible hope syndrome.

Sometimes I think Tom finds a disturbance of plans harder to take than I do. Ever since his accident, he has listened to my medical reports with outrage. "If *you* decide!" he stormed today. "Why doesn't *he* decide?" He paced the room. The doctor knows that I believe the decision should be nature's, that a baby should be born at its *own* time, not to suit his convenience or mine. But he leaves for his conference in Chicago day after tomorrow. If labor begins during his absence, the consultant will deliver the baby. But he could perform a Cesarean tomorrow, if I decide in favor of it. "What is he doing to you?" Tom raged. "What kind of man *is* he?"

And outdone by my own involvement, I cried, "A monstrous academician!"

Tom couldn't stay in the house after a few more minutes. He said he had an appointment with a student, but I know he simply had to get away from me. He is so eager to *do* something that he would go and dig up the Parthenon if it would help me, but as there is nothing to be done, he must go out and walk off his emotion. I know this; nevertheless, as soon as he was gone I burst into hot tears of resentment.

If only the winter would end! But there was another frost last night. My lichens outside the door, the orange wax and green bristle, are blighted, and have retreated underneath their strips of bark. And now, like nearly everyone else we know, we have caught a winter virus. Mine has sunk into my chest, and I have coughed all morning. And my mother has telephoned to report she has it too.

A dignitary visiting the campus without his wife has created what is viewed here as a need for a stag party. Tom doesn't want to go for fear my labor may begin. But there is a lecture tonight that I want to hear, and so he has decided to look in on the party for an hour while I am away. Anyhow, it would be easy enough to walk the few blocks to the hospital or take a taxi should the need arise, and for once I feel like getting out. That is a warning sign, I'm told: a burst of energy often precedes labor. Nevertheless, it seems most unlikely. Tom says he'll probably be back first.

But of course he is not here. Of course? I know what has happened. He has become engrossed in conversation and failed to notice the time. Conversation! Must he *talk?* When I got back and saw that there was no light in the living room, I came straight to the bedroom to try to read. But it is impossible. I am trembling with anger. For the first time in all these weeks, I have felt like getting out of the house. And yet we have drifted so far from a concern for each other that it didn't occur to us to be together. He is sick of my self-preoccupation. And I am sick of his sociability. Twice this week friends of his from the campus have dropped by without warning. He knows that I abhor chance visitors, but he encourages them. I know that tonight I urged him to go out. I know that I reasonably spoke of walking alone to the hospital. But now I am enraged.

It is almost eleven now. A gnawing stir has possessed me for more than an hour. It has only just struck me that it may be the onset of labor. I must watch the clock to see how frequently it occurs.

Past midnight. The pains cannot be timed. Two came at an interval of fifteen minutes, but then a **137** half-hour passed without another sign. Perhaps they are only a product of my anger. Or my imagination. We are sure to have a dreadful quarrel.

By the time he got home last night, the sensations had stopped. Undoubtedly, they were what the doctor calls "practice contractions." My anger had made me as rigid as a post, and when I heard the front door I turned to a column of marble. He had brought someone with him, someone very drunk. Niño barked at that outrage, as he barks at any stranger. They tried to quiet him. There were stumblings, and finally it sounded as if our guest had kicked the dog. He yelped, and Tom thrust him into the bedroom without a glance at me. He was confident that I was asleep. His companion's voice reached me, utterly inarticulate. He should have been taken home to bed, but was instead being served a nightcap. At length I heard Tom's cheery, "Drop around anytime!" and the front door closed. I wrenched on the reading lamp and spoke with bitter irony: "I think your friend needs attention. Shouldn't you walk him home?"

He came in, surprised by my voice and not too sober himself, to lavish remorse upon the dog. Had he been hurt? Let's see that paw. It was enough to break my marble column into a hail of stones. I seized them and hurled at random. I lied. Labor had begun, I said. But why hadn't I telephoned him? He had left a number. Hadn't I seen it? He went into the living room for proof and returned with a note he had left beside the telephone. Or course I hadn't seen it. It only made me angrier. He hadn't mentioned that he meant to leave the number. Then the necessity of retreating from my lie and confessing that the "labor" was false made me angrier still. I took the dog from him and said, "Oh, leave us alone, won't you?" What murderous justice I felt!

And he felt the same. Yes, probably he shouldn't have let anyone so drunk go off alone like that. He would see that good friend home. He would hear no more of this!

The front door slammed. His rage exploded in unrhythmic footfalls down the street. But soon he returned, like some large and baffled creature shunted by instinct, and flung himself upon the couch. He thought I might be needing help, I know.

How he sleeps! I thought, feeding my anger its breakfast. And it had lunched before he woke.

But when I took Niño for his noonday walk, the night's events were shrouded by a sense of unreality. The angry words were out and could not be recalled. They had escaped me altogether. Perhaps that is what saves us from the danger in a quarrel. If belief in it persists, it is something to worry about. Like death. All the while he was in the hospital, I couldn't believe in the possibility of his death.

There has been a thaw. The streets glittered with dampness caused by the sun. My lichens on the front stoop have thrust up their persistent tentacles again.

Perhaps no marriage could survive except for this mutability of human emotion. There are, of course, *139* some characters that just go stiff and stay so until the life they are connected to unquickens. And to marriage they are fatal, and if they attain some social power they are a danger, like witches whom devils will not release. But most people are more like us, subject to random demons that soon pass on to riper subjects. I know their work. They prey especially on loneliness. A person who wakes up alone for a cold gray stretch of days must spend some part of every morning undoing the diabolic knot inside. City people, who more often live alone than others, will call it morning anxiety, to be undone at times only by the second or third lunchtime cocktail. But they are not always exempt from more palatable relief. They too know love, and the demons move on. Loneliness is not exclusive to the solitary dweller, and, as everybody knows, the devils' delight is in complexity. Let some cloud of loneliness settle on a man for just an evening, and his mate may hear vindictive voices: Punish him, punish him. And given a hearing where they know they cannot thrive, they speak with more insistence: Turn him out! Tell him to leave you alone!

A man may go, but he'll come back to drive the devils from his house. Our modern witch doctors with their game of Viennese checkers have a term: Adjustment. How flat and unsatisfactory, like most of their work! Let them learn Exorcism, if they would be useful, and forget Adjustment of the household furniture, which only admits space behind some chest or footstool for the demon breeding ground.

I'll be no breeder of demons, I thought. When I got back, he had left for a faculty meeting, and on the desk I found the note on which he had written the number the night before. It was scratched out, and underneath was a new set of numbers, the words "until one," and a single word of love.

I have let out a flood of raging tears alone. It was infinitely relaxing. Such anger needs no object. Why must I look for one? It is what I should have done weeks ago, just after the accident. It made me angry. At the time, I wrote: "No one is to blame. It makes us feel worse." But even against ill chance you can't hold a grudge for long before it bites you. It is a demon to be turned loose, in a relief of solitary rage if need be. I think I have inhibited my feelings because of some silly fear of harming the baby. Of course, tension is more harmful than tears.

In the game of Viennese checkers, marbles are held up for free association. The marble "love" will often evoke the matchmate "hate" I'm told. It is love's inseparable enemy and its natural ally. Men have often insisted, their actions notwithstanding, that the species aims at perfection of itself, and I would beg the question further and insist that it must be found in what we learn to do with love and hate. The world at large stands far from knowing how to reconcile those two, but it may be learning that it must try. We know hatred is a positive corrective. *141*

Without it, who would have the drive to right injustice, who would bother to storm the Bastille, organize labor, or sit-in at some shabby greasy spoon? Without it, who would consult his conscience? Or speak to his love of what is not lovable between them?

Little one waiting for your turn, I'd like a better world to bring you to. Perhaps I only invert the wistful hope that you yourself may make it better, like the mother who hopes her child's brilliant marriage may save her from the poorhouse. You have, to start with, only what *we* are, your father and I, and our own (we think not negligible) resources for treating home truths. They are cutting, often. But we shall always try to see both edges of the blade and grasp it in the middle. Parents don't usually bring their children grievances against each other, but praise, and children guess the blame, meeting at a tender age love's inseparable enemy.

Many people live their lives out trying to come to terms with the opposing strength within them, and others merely float on the surface of the struggle, neither reaching down to it nor feeling its tug—much. But no human can be exempt from it and remain human. To everyone the Creation is enacted and the Fall is followed shortly by the conflict of the brothers. Our inheritance is to turn upon ourselves. You may find that as a legacy it doesn't amount to much. Perhaps you may be the one who masters it by some prodigious leap beyond that conflict. But leap, my 142 child, or fight. Don't float upon the surface.

And now I shall go lift the windows to clear the air, and then encourage the lichens with a jug of water.

Something about the accident was lingering on the fringes of my mind, but I didn't catch hold of it until I had gone outside with the water jug. Perhaps I had to drop the water jug in order to catch it.

In the clumsiness of getting my bulk outside the door while keeping the dog inside, I lost my footing and took a fall, tripping on the stoop. I was jarred to the sidewalk. I cried out, more in surprise than pain, and remained on my knees, listening to a thump beneath my heart, before I noticed that the water jug lay under my left hand, in pieces. Some of the fragments were covered with blood from the palm of my hand. And there nearby were the lichens, in their damp strips of bark, knitting out their cooperative existence, surviving in their own rootless world. I thought: I must get to Tom. But there was no need. He had seen this small event from a distance down the street. I heard his footsteps break into a run.

In the subsequent minutes, while he led me into the bathroom, turned the cold-water tap upon the palm of my hand, and picked the fragments of glass out of it, my mind reeled back to that evening on the country pike, where it struck and crashed against a culvert, and spilled in terrible pain onto the snowy roadbank. I had awakened to that crash, unable to decide if it had been a dream, and instead of running **143** out to see—the road was long and cold—I had only waited. Until now, the crash had never been my own.

Only as he held my hand against the flow of cold water did I really come to feel the unalterable mingling of our blood. Our ceremony of love had not completely persuaded me, nor had the knowledge of this spiral chain of cells I bear quite convinced me, that the harm that comes to another human being also comes to me. I have become linked irrevocably to a pattern of other lives in a way that happened to me only once before, at birth. And it can be truly ended in only one way, at death. I have been slow to come to this discovery, in its terror and its grace.

So much in the two of us complements and corresponds that I had not yielded to dependence, or even considered, without an uneasy shame, the single secret we have kept from each other. We have often marveled at the absence of secrecy between us. What histories we each survived to come together never trouble us, although in this first year we've seldom spelled out details. We are no pickers of dead fruit in the winter orchard. But now there is no need even for that single secret, and I let it out as he bound my hand with gauze. "You love me more," I said.

He spoke some reassurance about my hand and went to make us both a drink. And when he brought the glass and set it before me, I knew his hand trembled not for what I had said but for fear that his reassurance might not have been true. He wonders if indeed there is nothing to fear for my health or for the child, a further evidence of the secret's truth. But

144

here is the paradox of the imbalance that disqualifies it as a threat to us: Mine would be the greater loss if we ever were to part.

It is the last day. The doctor's journey to Chicago has passed without event. I have telephoned to report that, and he has persuaded me to allow him to perform the operation tomorrow, for he believes that I am several weeks overdue. I still have a resistance to rushing a baby into the world before it gives some sign of being ready, but the doctor assures me that belief in "a time to be born" is false idealism. His schedule, not his assurances, persuaded me at last. He leaves for his next speaking engagement the day after tomorrow and will be gone all week.

Thinking to be kind, friends have called us several times tonight to invite us to spend the evening with them. They say they know how I feel. They say other cheerful and encouraging things. They insist that we come. But I want only the help from the hand that reaches for mine as I awake. And Tom says he wants only to spend the evening alone here. "You're so beautiful," comes the tender, heartfelt lie. My Tom. I'll make it all up to you one day.

Tonight we are lighthearted, thanks to having remembered a letter Tom wrote me a year ago. I said something to him about everything's being upside down, head-over-heels, and he smiled. "Do you remember my linguistic exercise on 'head-over-heels'?" I took it out and read it again, a love letter, whimsical and fond, in diagrammatic academese: "Reinterpre-   *145* tation of Culturally Common Utterance (Cliché): 'I-am-head-over-heels-in-love,' a chart of morphemes marked by juncture and tone contour, a demonstration of the type thought to be elegant in linguistic circles."

The letter, written from Mexico, reminded me again of that day on the hillside, when I had felt the twinge of impatience that presaged the shift my life would take. I put it back with the others. I'll read them all again one day soon. He often spoke in them of fathering my children. Just the sight of those letters, proudly and exuberantly sentimental, cancels out the lingering disappointment about tomorrow's schedule. When they were written, we had not begun to live any of the plans they were so full of. . . .

PART THREE

The hospital's new wing is a cylinder like the Guggenheim Museum, and the floor where the mothers abide, an amphitheater. The mothers are in adjacent glass rooms, like opera boxes, from where we look out upon the center stage. The wing is joined to the old part of the hospital by a long corridor, through which the babies pass several times a day, for they live in a place no longer new, apart from the mothers. Here, there is no "rooming-in," the revolutionary system in which the care of the young by the mother is undertaken. The babies live in a band together, in quarters that are desegregated, although their mothers' quarters are not. Presumably, babies are less sensitive than their mothers to color, and require no special treatment for it. There are three Negro babies in the nursery among about a dozen whites. One, however, *is* separate, having been born unequal, premature. He lies isolated in his sterile cage, too small to look upon for very long, and makes no stir. I have seen the nursery, traveled the length of the corridor, and entered my glass box. I look out now, through a picture window, upon the arena. Should the action there grow wearisome, a television set suspends above the window for alternate fare. I am eager, though, for the live performance to begin.

There are continuous showings, and, like the setting, the play is both classic and modern. First, I notice the chorus. It is made up of young girls, novices, student nurses, clad in costumes of tiny blue and white checks. They whisper and, yes, giggle together, and carry news around the arena, for they have no regular post. They stand on the fringe of activity, outside the circular white counter that sets off the central stage. Those costumed in white enter there. They are older nurses for the most part. But occasionally men move into that round. They walk behind the counter and speak to the women in white. They write upon pads and read what others have written, and then move away to one of the glass compartments where a mother waits. All attend their word and watch for their sign, for they are the mothers' medicine men.

Now and then a mother herself enters that arena, like a character from an *avant-garde* play who leaves the audience to invade the action. She is dressed in colored slippers and robes to do a dance of life. Her step is sleepy and slow, her face suffused with such delight as to suggest she may have dined upon the mystic mushroom and glimpsed eternity. On her second day there, she promenades about the circle once.

On the third, twice, and so on for each of her days before she leaves.

We walked to the hospital, only half a dozen blocks, no more than I have walked every day, but it took thirty minutes. The wind had become so strong that I could scarcely push against it. An uncanny blackness had settled over the afternoon, and we still had a block to go when the first rain splashed in heavy gouts. My virus had affected me like hay fever, with which I've never been troubled, and I sniffled disgustingly. My hip caught with every step. I asked, "Have you ever walked so slowly, Tom?" and he laughed:
"Never."

I said, "It's almost over now," but I didn't believe it. Somehow I think I shall always have this maimed tread. I have forgotten what it was like to be slender. I used to take pride that my figure looked so young, but now it seems impossible that it can ever be restored. Such a thing is not within the range of my ambition. Now I long only for relief. From the broad glass pane behind my bed there comes a cruel grayness, from which now and again a sudden light erupts. The rain falls in soundless streaks against the insulated glass.

"It's an electric storm," said Miss Willie, "and you know what that means." No, I said, I didn't know. Miss Willie wears the blue- and white-check costume that identifies her as a student nurse. She is a blonde with delicate coloring and the pleasant contrast of robust flesh. Her lips are inexperienced and eager, but her eyebrow arches worldly-wise. "Brings on labor, old wives say. You'll see, too. We'll have more deliveries tonight than we've had all week. That bed will not be empty long." She nodded to the other bed in my room, now unoccupied. I have a semiprivate opera box.

Miss Willie invited me to "pop on the scales to show how small you are." Her manner annoyed my husband, but I don't mind her. When she left us alone for a few minutes, I told him that southern women have a way of flirting with each other. It is true. Tom left soon, at four o'clock, when visiting hours ended, and I found I had already begun to fall in with Miss Willie's manner. I told her she must be careful to follow the special instructions about my preparation, and she went to the outer arena to look them up. My doctor had agreed to modify the cleansing rite for me, as a concession to my belief that certain aseptic measures will one day be as obsolete as the application of leeches. Miss Willie returned almost at once and said there were no special instructions and that she must proceed by the book. I held my ground, however, and, still within the form of our feminine flirtation, sent her off to her superior. She returned shortly to say that we must wait until the night supervisor came on. She stayed for a few minutes, seeing to my needs and taking my blood pressure. She asked if I was hoping for a boy or a girl, and I said I didn't care.

There was a brilliant flash of light, and Miss Willie laughed. "I hope you don't go into labor. It's bad luck for a C-section to come in during a storm. I wouldn't know how to take that baby, if you were to drop it here. I never delivered." But she has witnessed delivery. "It's wonderful," she said with a keen tone of surprise. "It wasn't at all like I expected." She had expected contractions, yes, and had imagined those. A nurse could feel those with her fingers, and follow by touch the progress of a labor. "But I thought you saw a couple of contractions, and then they did an episi-otomy, and then the baby would just come. But it's not that way at all." I urged her to be explicit, and as she spoke her voice grew animated by a specific mem-ory. "Well, *everything* contracts, not just the womb. There's this dilation, you see. There's room enough all of a sudden for—well, think of a fair-sized orange," she tried lamely. "When I saw the baby's head come into that space—you just wouldn't *believe* what it's like to see that head come out!"

"What *is* it like?"

"Oh, like . . ." A remembered elation lit up her eyes, but her lips pressed each other in frustration. "I wish I could *say!*" she cried.

Thus, the poet, with a dream his language can-not equal. Miss Willie stood looking out upon the rain for several moments before she shook her head and shrugged in rueful resignation.

The night supervisor has come in and thwarted my eccentric aim of avoiding one of the two ritual baths. There is one at night and one just before the delivery. She had received no special instructions, and *151* with tactful calm explained what I already knew: that patients are admitted a night in advance of surgery for just this purpose. She has that elusive balance between order and compassion essential to a good nurse, and betrayed no disapproval or wonder at my wayward theories. There was nothing to do but submit with what grace was left me. Besides, it gave Miss Willie something to think about other than the failure of her descriptive powers. She plunged with zeal into the practical task at hand. We were respectfully silent, Miss Willie and I, as she prepared the morrow's sacrifice. Then after, cleansed, drained, shorn, I lay upon the block and was fed a dinner labeled Liquid. Somehow, it was all very soothing.

I am glad to have known Miss Willie as she is now, for by the time she finishes her training she will have learned professional restraint and will no longer try to explain some experience with life to a chance patient. Nor will she dare, as she did before she left me, agree that part of any rite is silly. Like the night supervisor, she will see the heightened emotion in the patient as a thing to meet rather less than halfway. The impersonal mode, as the most reasonable insurance for survival, will have become her second nature. The regimen admits of no morbidity, and is designed to discourage any such tendency in the patient. And yet, there is a perverse effect created by this very sterility, control, whiteness. One can fairly see the dying microorganisms, among chaos, in the dark. Every mo-

152

ment seems vivid as it is lived, sharpened by the certainty of mortality. Even in a maternity section, where you are fairly sure of getting out not only with your own life but with another one as well, you feel quickened by some unearthly excitement. Truth becomes something palpable, very near. It seems to approach you, and you believe that with a little effort you might reach out and touch it and hold it fast.

Now that the lights in my glass box are lowered, and the performers in the arena are reduced to two, who scarcely move before the sleeping audience, I want somehow to get free enough from my fatigue to think a little, of my husband, of tomorrow, of the child. I am alone, as I shall perhaps never again be for a long while. The lightning fills the room with a short glare. The rain washes the glass. I want so much to think, but I can feel instead that the sensible side of the regimen will prevent it, for I have taken the sleeping potion. The will may be stirred to explore the heart and its desires, but can do no more than toss, turn, and then submit to the body's need. Besides, how sweet it is at last, after such long wakefulness, to sleep. . . .

The brisk schedule of the morning is under way now. The storm is over. But while it still raged last night, at some early hour, the other bed in my room was prepared for a patient who had arrived in labor. A nameplate, "Mrs. Mary Dante," hangs from her bed. I awoke to hear that she was then in "L & D,"

Labor and Delivery. As a "C-section," I am to be spared that, the visit to those bleak, cramped rooms we saw last month.

During the daytime, there is little rest to be had in a hospital, except for a temperament that runs by the clock. That fortunate will perhaps discover the half-hour periods when nothing is scheduled: no blood-pressure and temperature takings, no breakfast or lunch, no morning dosings, no visitors. The lady technician returns the thermometer to its bin and leaves, only to make way for the minor medicine men, the interns, making their rounds. They come two by two, and tap and pry. Then comes a "chief" resident, who repeats many of their questions. Then, shortly, the "head" medicine man, my own doctor, appears. He tells me he has ordered more X rays, to see if the bronchial infection has spread. The time of the operation has been changed. It will be later than one o'clock—he doesn't know exactly when. But it must be over before three-thirty, when he has a conference of some sort. I had hoped it would be over before Tom's two o'clock seminar, but perhaps it will only be beginning then.

Two more inquisitors have arrived just now, young women wearing sea-green robes, and sea-green paper shower caps over their hair. One of them I recognized when she spoke. The deep brown pupils of her eyes seemed to reflect a state of perpetual excitement. "We're going to be taking care of your baby in

154

the nursery," she said, "and we have a few questions."
It was she who had stopped me in the hallway that
day I came to the first mothers' class. "The babies are
out," she had asserted enigmatically, and then I realized she meant out of the nursery. Here was the same
slender elf, all in her costume of sea green. How personally pleased she seemed that my baby was nearly
"out" and in her care. Yes, I told her, I expect to
breast-feed. Oh, excellent, the eager brown eyes said.
Yes, it is my first baby. Really? I seemed too calm for
it to be a first. The nurse who brings the baby for feeding, she explained, will give me whatever help I may
need. She explained that some mothers need a good
deal of help, others very little. I hoped fervently that
I shall need very little. She smiled and went back
down the hallway to the place where the babies stay.
Is it living among babies that keeps her eyes so wondering and wide?

During these morning ceremonies, Mrs. Dante
has been wheeled in from the delivery room. She
wears a rubber tube taped to her arm that allows the
passage into her veins of some nourishing solution.
She is pale and lovely, and lies now in a sedated sleep.
The nurse had a question or two for her when she first
came in: "Are you comfortable now?" To which Mrs.
Dante gave the vague response, "No more ... no
more." Then: "Are you glad it was a boy?" And to
that, her voice gave a faint but chilling reply: "A boy,
yes. If I was a boy, I'd be safe." She asked for ice, *155*

which the nurse provided wrapped in a cloth. Then, pressing the ice to her dry lips, Mrs. Dante closed her eyes again, murmuring, "No more . . . no more."

I can feel no effect from the sedative I have taken. My cough is still very active. I am heavy, leaden. I have been X-rayed, have taken a liquid lunch, have seen my husband. It is an hour before the child will be born. *You don't call that a birth, do you?* I close my eyes, and see Mrs. Drummond's kind, mad face. That's right, dear lady, the Cesarean child has a performance, not a birth. The operation is performed at a man-made time. How can such a thing command the respect, or even the name, of a birth? In the X-ray department, a girl with violet eyes, a technician, waited with me until my turn came. And while we waited, another young woman in a white coat introduced herself. The anesthesiologist. She said she wanted to talk to me about my anesthetic before the operation. This was merely a courtesy visit, as of course she will do what the doctor has ordered. Perhaps the doctor has sent her, to help overcome my mistrust of anesthetics, for she is personable, but there is no need for further reassurances now that I have yielded to diagnosis. "Is it your first baby?" she asked, and I nodded. The technician's violet eyes widened. "Your first baby! And you'll have it today? But you're so calm, I can hardly believe it's your first!" I suggested that it may be different if you don't have the excitation of labor, but still she shook her head and smiled with a shy, floral gaze. She too wanted to know whether I wanted a boy or a girl. How can anyone believe it makes a difference?

Back here in the arena theater, I have talked to Mrs. Dante. She is remarkably revived, and has eaten a full lunch marked Solid. "Just when that storm was at its worst," she told me, "I got down to business and started pushing. I didn't labor with this one but an hour and a half." The new son was her eighth child. She had not wanted so many, she said, but as they came along, she loved each one. And yet, each time she found herself hoping it was the last. Her voice, so faint before lunch, is now merely soft and gentle. She has just astonished me by shoving back her tray, tossing her legs over the side of the bed, and sliding her feet to the floor. She has walked to the bathroom with a confident, if careful, step. Before she closed the door, she asked, "Are you in labor? You're so calm." And when I explained myself, she said, "Even so, you're awful calm." She is the third person to wonder at my composure. And then she asked, inevitably, "Do you want a boy or girl?"

All at once, I realize I am not calm. I can scarcely write. It's almost over, it's almost over!

How curious those last words seem to me now. *It's almost over.* Such backward-looking words, taking no account of what was about to happen. No wonder the women had marveled at my calm; I had simply begun to wait for an end, like a prisoner with no no- *157* tion of what would come with liberation. I had served my term, and at the end I had no thought for the voluntary bondage I would so soon embrace.

It is like another theater. The cast arrives in order of importance. The nurses are scrubbing up when the patient appears, scarcely noticed, rather like a maid with a duster. Then, following the entrances of an intern and the anesthesiologist, the action begins slowly, with some traditional exposition. Last to make an entrance is the star of the performance, the doctor. One almost expects a round of applause.

There is great economy of motion, for the players are well rehearsed. Improvised action would be banished. The mood is set for comedy, highly stylized. It is a sternly disciplined troupe, which can doubtless turn less jocose given a more sober theme. But, cheerful and cheering, they smile and persuade smiles.

I felt myself both bit player and director of this performance, the one because I had so little to do and the other because everyone consulted me. Did I feel comfortable? Was that position of the arm all right? They were so gentle, I scarcely realized that *they* and not *I* induced my immobility. In a hospital, we become more egotistical than ever. Seeing that the intern, who happened to be Chinese, held a needle, I suggested to him the vein I thought best suited to receive it, and watched the satisfactory ascent of a tube like Mrs. Dante's from my hand up to the bottle of sugar water hooked above my head. And then I saw to the taping of my hand to a splint to keep it from any sudden jarring movement. Next, the anesthesiologist

158

received direction. She made an attempt to keep her props, drug supplies and horse needle, beyond the range of my vision, and she was a sensitive performer. She prepared the spot where her needle would be inserted with such skillful timing that when the doctor made his entrance there was not a moment lost.

Like the others, the doctor wore a costume of sea green. When did hospital white undergo this transformation? He seemed taller than ever in his long straight gown, and moved with such a spring that I had to look at his feet. He wore sterile white cloth overshoes tied at the ankle. The effect was to lend him the bounce of an athlete. All in all, he was younger, and free almost completely of his everyday academic style. I felt that glow of satisfaction a director always enjoys from excellence in a performer. I was proud of my casting. His entrance gave a measurable lift to the other players, who turned to him as if he were the sun. I would surely get the best that everyone had to give on the occasion of this opening.

I abdicated my control, as a wise director will with a superior artist, and relaxed to enjoy my role as bulky bit player. It was my moment now, for I had been placed in a fetal position by the others. At a nod from the doctor, the anesthesiologist made the injection into the deadened spot, and there was a light crunch of needle upon bone. Then, once more stretched full length, I was divided in two by a sea-green sheet. From one side, I watched the circle of masked faces intent upon the other side.

"My mask fell off," I remarked. I had just re- *159*

membered that when I came in I too had been unable
to breathe, had in turn wriggled my mouth free from
the mask, and someone had simply taken it away.
Was that because half of me is immune to the germs
of the other half? If so, why mask me at all? I suspect
the mask had served its ceremonial end and that all
might as freely go unmasked, except that the play
would lose some of its mystery. At that awful thought,
I realized the meaning of a numb pressure. "Another
ritual bath?" I asked the medicine man, who changed
the subject with a sly smile.

"She's an awfully good patient," he said to the
anesthesiologist, who agreed. This is a litany, meant
to appease any hostile element.

And then there came a moment of transition, in
which the doctor glanced over the curtain at my face.
And theater, ritual, illusion—all hung in perfect balance in that moment. Some words were exchanged
between us, the substance of which I have forgotten.
What we said we spoke lightly, a reassurance: yes,
we are confident and ready to begin. And then, illusion gave place to reality. The comedy became the
thing it stood for. No symbol remained, only life itself.

I watched the face of a dark nurse. Mature and
lean, it showed some history of strain. The eyes that
looked for instructions from the doctor had circles
under them and a fine mesh of lines, but the eyes
themselves were brightly attentive. The clock behind
her advanced five minutes. And then there came the
sound of suction, and the dark nurse, after a look of

inquiry at the doctor, bent down beside the sea-green sheet with swift intent.

"It's a boy," she said. "You have a boy."

There was no time for thought to form. What came was something more like reflex, a deep stir of pride, tribal and involuntary. In that moment, whatever my civilized self may know, I believed beyond a doubt that every woman must passionately hope her firstborn will be a son.

So many moments pass from our living memory. Often those we want to keep, knowing their meaning and importance, will yield to some lesser moment. For some reason, we may remember the warmth from the kitchen stove as a kind aunt dressed us for an ordinary winter day, and forget the wild elation from some rare birthday or Christmas treat. For the life of me, I cannot call up the magic of a certain youthful rapture that inspired a hundred pages of wastepaper rhymes, but can at once revive the cold, reckless delight of a swim I took with some indifferent fellow in a clear volcanic lake said to be bottomless. Shall I perhaps forget the emotions of this day, my son, in favor of some future minor joy?

You appeared before me, so secure in the support of our doctor's lean hand that it was quite invisible. You alone were there, pale and composed, your flesh undisturbed by the short journey you had just made, even though it was the most important of your life. Yellow moisture clung to the down of your tiny forehead, and yet your brown hair, so surprisingly abundant, curled dry, close against your ears. Your fists were pressed at your chest as if you did not yet know you could open out the fingers. It was the movement of your lips that most impressed me. They curved in a small bow. You seemed to turn your head—although it must have merely bobbed away from the finger bracing it—and as it moved your lips curled upward in discovery, suddenly aware of the feel of some new element. Your tongue made a smack inside, and your lips parted and admitted your first breath of life. You sucked the air inside, and released it with a vocal sound.

At that, you were given over to some other supporting hand, and the moment was at an end. I could not at first see where you had gone. I looked about, and instead of you I saw the faces of the others in the room. I knew none of the people there, except our doctor, and yet I could see that behind their masks everyone was smiling. I realized then that everyone smiles at a birth. The species rejoices in itself.

Everyone smiles. And yet, no one really knows the rapture in the mother but herself. It is hers alone, never quite to be imagined by the others, even by her child, unless perhaps on the day his own is born. I marvel at it. One half of me was quite insensate, and yet I felt united by a total, physical wonder. It must then be a thing outside any human explaining, at one with the miracle of birth itself.

The doctor had turned back to the longer part of his operation, but I wanted him to know just what

I felt. I fixed upon the infant utterance. "Did you

hear what the baby said? He said 'la.' " The doctor spared me a glance of moderate interest, but he seemed to miss the deep importance I attached to the palatal sound. I thought of my student nurse, Miss Willie, and knew her frustration: "If *only* I could say . . ." I urgently wanted him to know how thoroughly I approved of him, even of his "academic objectivity." I said I had believed that what I was feeling came as a reward of labor, almost like relief. He shook his head, oh, no, a little cool now, as if wary of my threatening display. And then it was not possible to remain intent upon what I wished to say, for a series of enraged cries reached me. In the corner, the baby was being washed by two interns just within the range of my eye. One of the interns nodded, smiling. "We'll bring him to you soon," he said. And then, scrubbed free of all sign of his embryonic life, the child was held before me, stiff with outrage, his hands opened now, uncurled. He remained there long enough to imprint a firm genetic proof: yes, his hair grew on his scalp in cowlicks exactly like his father's.

I wanted to touch that head, and only then did I realize that my hand, the one not engaged in receiving the liquid through a needle, was under some subtle restraint. Even now I can't remember what stopped me, for I couldn't move my eyes away from the baby for the second it would take to glance at my hand. Perhaps someone was merely holding it to keep me from disturbing the doctor.

And then the baby was taken away, and the doctor was speaking to me, and I forgot again about my hand. "They washed him," I said, interrupting. "Among the Hari they butter the baby." But the doctor didn't care about the Hari. He cared about the side discoveries he was making. Suddenly he leaned over the sea-green curtain with something else in his hand, the placenta, all purple and gold. He said, "It's really quite beautiful, I think." Yes, a royal infant robe. Yes, beautiful. Everything is beautiful. I heard and saw through a dreamy acquiescence. Then he nodded to the anesthesiologist, and in seconds my new term of life was under way. It was indeed over, and I was free. Except of the vision of that sovereign being, unlike any other alive, new, priceless, mine.

Mrs. Dante said, "Lord, honey, I don't mind you coughing. When you have seven at a table and one in a crib, a little cough won't trouble your dreams." But the fact is that I have just waked her up for the second time this afternoon. She added, "When they can move me into one of the four-bed rooms, there'll be a lot more distraction than you can make, so don't you worry." She has told me that she will save two dollars a day if space in the more crowded room becomes available. They brought her baby in a few minutes ago and pulled the curtain between us. Only the mother is allowed to be with the baby while it nurses, a hygienic measure that has the fringe benefit of giving them a few minutes of privacy.

When the nurse came back for him, Mrs. Dante turned to me. "As soon as they take hold, you don't ever want them to let go," she said. But her wide brown eyes were clouded with worry. "I guess God'll help us make room some whichway."

I was coughing again, and she leaned up on an elbow in concern. "They might of waited a couple of days on you, I think, until that cleared up. Sounds to me like you got a rattlesnake in your chest."

The cough has only begun to reassert itself now that the anesthetic has worn off. I wasn't aware of it at all during the four hours in the Recovery Room.

Perhaps I didn't cough there. Perhaps I didn't moan either. It may have been those others in the other beds. I could see them from time to time. There must have been about twenty of them, and when they lifted their heads, as many did, writhing, I could see them. For the most part, though, I saw only the intravenous bottles nodding above the beds. From time to time the curtains would sweep around the beds the way they do here in our semiprivate opera box. Only, here they do it for privacy, and there they seemed to do it in order to muffle an especially loud sound. Once I awoke aching, to find that a curtain had been swept around my own bed and that bars had risen about its sides as if to cage in some clawing wildcat. For the most part, though, all the curtains were open and the bottles were nodding, as were the heads of many attendants as they wafted in and out. Everyone passed before my eyes, faded and returned, everyone I already knew, the doctors, interns, and nurses, and a few I had not seen before. And high above everybody's head, a clock seemed to magnetize my memory every half-hour. It was never to end, I thought; I would writhe forever below those nodding bottles and nodding heads. The advance of the half-hours seemed to prove that in some way.

Next to me a man was moaning horribly. His bed was no more than two feet from mine. I could have reached out to comfort him. He was gray in every fiber, gray hair, gray skin, but very handsome. He writhed and trembled. Did he feel the same way I felt? Many attendants hovered over him from time to time. I asked someone, "Has he had a baby?" The bars rose at his sides and the curtains closed about him, but still his groans were audible through the cloth. Would he die? I wondered. Everywhere, a kind of collective unconscious seemed to be surfacing and then sinking, as if frightened away by groans.

At the next turn of the clock a new face appeared, one I'd never seen before. She stood tall on very slender legs and wore a distinguished suit of brown. She introduced herself as the pediatrician. How nice; unlike the other doctors, she shunned a uniform. She was gray-haired and had rather sad brown eyes. She spoke with swift warmth—where had I heard that accent before? "The baby looks fine. Very healthy." Oh, now I remember: it is a manner of speech peculiar to well-born southern women who have had a Yankee education and returned home for their career. The tongue and temperament are distinctly southern. Rapid and clipped, yet more elided than the slowest drawl. She left without my knowing it, and another half-hour turned.

Now the face before mine was beautiful, young, kind, utterly trustful. Its eyes were green, darkly fringed, patient. "I am going to be your nurse tomorrow." Ah. She was off duty now. It was she who made me believe that the parade of half-hourly visitors was part of a plan to pull the patient back into consciousness, though someone said the room was so centrally located for the convenience of doctors and nurses. Anyway, I loved the green-eyed girl at once, with a firm, sisterly devotion. I explained that although I had been there for some hours, I didn't know if my husband had heard of the birth of his son. Or if my mother had heard. She would find out at once, she said, and vanished, whereupon the clock turned again.

The obstetrician appeared somewhere in this phantasmagoric dance of the half-hours, probably after his conference. I told him that he was higher than the bottles, although no one else was. He laughed and told someone I couldn't see to check me again in half an hour. I thought: I am receiving the best of all possible modern medical care. But what I said betrayed an ungracious turn of mind: "This place must be the latest thing in snake pits." He laughed again and faded away.

And then, at last, there was Tom, who bent down so that his eyes were on a level with mine. He took my hand. Yes, he said, he had telephoned my mother; she knew. And he had seen the baby, still rigid with rage, as he was wheeled in his box past the waiting room. And, oh, yes, Mrs. Drummond had been with *167* him at the time, just as she had promised. I remember thinking it was only a gesture when she'd said she wanted "to sit with him." She had no need to come all the way from the country for just the few minutes of the operation. Besides, to her it wasn't even a birth. "She came and sat with you?" I asked, touched beyond belief. "Yes, she came. And you know what? She didn't have a thing to say. She'd start a story and then she'd just stop. It happened over and over. At last she looked at me and said, 'I've gone and dried up.'" He told me that he kissed her at the end.

Last night, some of Mrs. Dante's large family were visiting her, among them her mother-in-law. I had been lying on my side, facing Mrs. Dante, and because I am not yet able to shift my weight without help, I was an inadvertent participant in the visit. The elder Mrs. Dante is white of hair and ample of breast, and, like her daughter-in-law, has a quick, responsive spirit. At my first cough she turned, full of sympathy, and half rose from her chair. I motioned her back to her seat. A word, and the cough rises in my chest. Why had no one come to pull the curtain so that the elder Mrs. Dante wouldn't be disturbed? Or rather, why couldn't I permit her, no, *ask* her, to sit beside me and hold me in her great peasant arms until the fit subsided?

In the end, late at night, one of the older nurses helped me. She had a breast as broad as the old Italian woman's, and she pressed me against it in such a way that I was forced to cough. The relief was indescribable, only one sharp pain at the incision. Why had I struggled against something so simple? But then, when it started over again, a younger and slenderer nurse came with advice instead of an embrace. I only made matters worse, she said, by trying *not* to cough. It was all up to me. I must give in to it. Give in, give in. But I am stiff with resistance. My will is too strong ever to give in.

Now, what in the name of heaven can I mean by that? My response to everything is irrational, overcharged. I am too much alive to life itself. Is that possible? This closed white world, pain, this refusal to give in—it is all unbearably vivid. I leak tears of self-pity.

I think now of the more old-fashioned nurse. She is overweight, and there are those who would be quick to explain her away with "psyche and glands." But at that quiet hour of the night, I saw justice in her and none other. She bears a marked resemblance to a cousin of mine, long dead now, whose name had in it the soft clinging sound of southern pampering— Alma Belle, Alma Belle. Yes, this nurse's mouth lifts in a thin curl as Cousin Alma Belle's did, and her hair lies in the same soft ringlets upon the folds of her plump neck. I even asked her if she had relatives in my home town, and when she said no, her eyes gave out the same blue twinkle of my cousin's. I can't remember that Alma Belle ever lent me the pillow of her breast—I'm sure that she did not. I haven't thought of her in years. But such ghosts as hers must wander through hospital halls at night, when, weak and retrograde, we want badly to give in, not to necessity but to some lost charity from childhood.

This afternoon, after his seminar, Tom brought a small object one of his students had made to illustrate a talk about the Tarahumara in northern Mexico. He wanted the other students to see the charm of this, the god's eye. It is nothing more than two small sticks and bits of pastel-colored yarn. The Tarahumara fashion a cross of the sticks, and at the center weave the yarn in a diamond shape in such a way that its design is a stylized eye. The threads are woven outward from the center, where the brown of the twig bark shows as a pupil, and the colors are pale pink and green and yellow. It is a soft, benevolent eye, but it is powerful. Kept in the home above a bed, it guards the family from unfriendly influences with a potency no human eye can equal. It can see dangers outside the family, to friend and tribe, threats from false gods that may assume a tempting and deceptive form. I attached the god's eye to a cord above my bed, and soon Mrs. Dante noticed it and asked to see it. She took it in her hand with a wondering smile and stared into the eye for quite some time before she passed it back. "I could use a thing like that," she said. "Maybe it could keep me from getting any more young uns."

Space has been made for Mrs. Dante in a four-bed room, and so someone new is in the opposite bed now, Mrs. Minna Jackson. She has just been delivered of a girl, her second, she told the nurse. She is carrying on a lively and lucid conversation with her mother right now. How envious she makes me! I can scarcely talk and am too tired even to want to see my baby.

Mrs. Jackson's conversation with her mother grew most candid, considering that she must know I could hear every word on the other side of my curtain. I rumbled my chest to warn her if she did not know. But she seemed not to care; or, rather, was too angry to care. "Dick's gone to work already? Earlier than he needs to, you know. He could be here. He's been a perfect pig this month." And although her mother's reply was a murmured attempt to change the subject, Mrs. Jackson's grievances were multiple and not to be suppressed. "It's a mess. What was the rush, Mother, will you tell me that? What in God's name were we in such a damn push about?" Another murmur. Then: "*You* were the pusher, you know it! I'd be on the dump heap at twenty-one if I didn't snap up Dick Jackson, remember? Oh, no, you didn't say 'dump heap,' but you know how you worried. You couldn't marry me off fast enough."

That outburst brought a more resolute voice from her mother. "Oh, Minna, honey, why don't you just rest. You're tired. You have a new little girl now. Isn't it enough to make you happy?"

But that only goaded her daughter: "Yes, another girl. So now I have to go through this all again, until we get a boy."

I wanted to tell her she needn't; that way madness lies. Must she go on and on like some dazed *171* woman at a slot machine in Reno? Her mother said, "Oh, Minna, baby, stop. You looked so lovely when they wheeled you in, and now your eyes are red."

Minna gave a short, explosive sigh. "All right, Mother. I was like this last time, remember? Just leave me alone a while."

Her mother said she'd make an appointment with the hairdresser down the hall for tomorrow. Here in the maternity section, where no one is really sick, there is a beauty shop. Minna said: "Oh, God, please do that. My hair's so sweaty. I'm a mess."

Now she has slept. A nurse has pushed back the curtain separating us, and I see that she is quite attractive and very young, not much more than twenty-one. Her features are sharply outlined, except for her mouth, which yields a wide, brilliant smile. However, her lips turn down when she speaks, in an ironic twist, as if to underline what she says. She has been chatting with some of the student nurses, whom she asked to help unpack her bag. They are enjoying themselves, for her lingerie is something to behold. Nylon gowns with clusters of appliquéd flowers, dusters of silk, a robe with a deep collar of rich lace. The girls have exclaimed over every piece as they folded them into the drawer. "They're nothing special," Mrs. Jackson said, as if she really meant it. Meanwhile, several pots of flowers arrived. She tapped the tag of one of them. "Mmm. My husband," she murmured. Her mouth took that ironic turn, and her eyes flickered without

pleasure.

But now she has spoken to a nurse in the most wistful of tones. "When can I see my baby, please? They gave me something just before she came that knocked me out. I wonder what she looks like. I haven't even seen her yet."

Nighttime here plays tricks on my unsteady mind. The first night there was the electric storm, the next night, the ghost of Cousin Alma Belle, and now, in the night just over, the predawn darkness has brought an apparition.

I awoke with the effort of stopping a cough, and sensed someone standing very close and looking down at me. But because it was that hour before the dawn, I could see nothing at first, until after a moment a nurse stirred beside the curtain at the foot of the bed. I can't remember ever having been so tired. What was she doing, standing there? Had I seemed to need help? I had been quiet, trying not to wake Mrs. Jackson. Then I saw the nurse was holding something, and with a start of fear I recognized it was my baby. She spoke, and though her voice was cheerful as the morning, I couldn't understand the everyday meaning in her words: "It's time for him, you know."

I only stared at her and shook my head, afraid. She shifted the blanketed form in her arms, and, seeing my condition, nodded as if she understood. Then she said, "Oh, you don't want him, do you?" And she vanished, although I called out, "Wait! *Give* him to me!" I could hear her retreating rubber-soled tread in the arena outside. Why, in that Greek theater, the nurse must have her own night visitors: the shades of the unnatural mothers—Andromache, Jocasta, Medea —would try her skill at withholding judgment. *Oh, you don't want him, do you?*

My calling out after the nurse awakened Mrs. Jackson, who asked what was wrong. I had gone to sleep with some hard thoughts toward her because she seemed to want nothing she had, and had acquired it too greedily and too soon. I feel less confident of that judgment now, somehow.

The nurse who took my morning temperature just now has explained the night visit. There is a feeding at six in the morning. But it wasn't necessary, she said, as babies are born with enough stored energy so that they do not become hungry until lactation begins several days after birth. She has left me all propped and pillowed, before a breakfast tray marked "Semi-Soft."

Tom's couvade is complete. He stood so long before the nursery window that the nurse brought him a chair. And when he came to me, I thought I had never seen such a look of wonder as touched his face. "It's the foot that gets me," he said. "He kicks the cover off so that this one foot sticks out. Exactly the way I do. My *habits* are built into him." I gave him a skeptical look, but only as an equalizer, for I too have seen it happen as I held the baby. The foot, small enough that it disappears if I fold my fingers about it, seeks exposure, no matter how carefully the nurses

wrap it up.

After having her hair done, Minna Jackson spent the rest of the morning on the telephone attending to a domestic crisis. When her mother arrived, she came in again for her share of the blame. "Didn't I *tell* you he'd get back at me about the station wagon?" she cried. Her husband had failed at the last minute to order their new washer-dryer. On the phone, Minna had learned that it had something to do with the payments on the old machine (which had no dryer), but she recounted nothing of her husband's explanation to her mother. Instead she said, "Now that I have my own car, I can go to the damn laundromat as far as he's concerned." But her mother still refrained from joining the attack upon her son-in-law. Instead, she opened a large dress box she had brought with her. It contained several new dresses for Minna's use when she leaves the hospital. They had an extremely salutary effect on her disposition. Minna was so cheerful by the time her mother was ready to leave that she asked to have the television set turned on.

But "things" have continued to prey upon her mind. Her pediatrician has just paid her a call. "Do you have a list of things the baby needs? I may have forgotten something since last time. What about a vaporizer? A friend of mine needed one of those when her baby caught a cold." The doctor suggested that she wait and see if her new baby was going to catch a cold or not. When he left, she looked thoughtful.

The consultant has just been here, in my doctor's absence. He has reminded me again of the limitations of this science of obstetrics and of how vital it is to *175* have confidence in one's doctor. I wish I had not called upon him, for I know he is a believer in statistics, which provide such convenient rules of thumb: "A section birth for any woman over thirty," for example. He listened to me with a cloudy southern gaze. I am, I explained reasonably, afraid of pain. This fear attaches to a set of muscles in the chest. A cough begins, tugging at the muscles of the incision, and then a defense against the cough starts up in the chest, to choke it down. At first, *I* controlled that defense; it delayed the cough. Now it is automatic, and results in spasms in the chest. A breathtaken panic sets in. It doesn't end until at last the deep cough breaks through. The cycle begins again almost at once, because the dread of it keeps me from relaxing.

The doctor shifted his weight, impatience flickering in his milk-blue eyes. (Here's one we've let go free, and yet she talks to me of pain.) He asked: "Why worry about it?" Plain upon his face was a desire to be shut of the unknown. The practitioner must treat what can be treated, otherwise he might go mad. Or into experimental research. After all, so little is understood of what emotion does to muscle, better give this the go-by. "Why worry about it?" is a good stock question, especially for women in labor who try to stop contractions. He knows that some women fight them and some do not. There's no explaining it. (Slip the mask over the little lady's face, and get her to go limp. It's the only way to deal with some of them. Now this, I guess it has to do with the psyche. Not my field.) I asked whether the second anesthetic that had put me out had been really necessary and whether I was not having a reaction to it.

The question seemed to please him somehow. He said: "There's something we call postpartum depression. . . . Oh, you've heard of it? Well, I'd say you're having it a little earlier than most." A satisfaction settled in his eyes, and he seemed unaware that he had accepted the descriptive term as an explanation. The words are like a chant of absolution and cover a multitude of sins. Postpartum depression: nearly every American woman has it. The fact is that since it is a term for certain effects of emotion upon muscle, very little is understood about it at all. Moreover, my question remains unanswered. But I have thanked him and swallowed his prescription. He could save somebody's life tomorrow, a fact which doubtless lets blacker consciences than his sleep well.

Tom has just left for the night. He tried to help me sort out the muscles that inhibit the cough. I am a hopeless weakling about pain, while he is a stoic. I cannot understand how he can be so patient and kind.

Last night a flash of lightning woke both me and my sleeping cough. Seeing that the glare had come from the television screen, I burst into tears of rage. All the other lights were out. How *dare* she watch the Late Show! Mrs. Jackson couldn't hear me, for she was listening to the sound track through her private earplugs. And so I was able to "give in" completely. The fury dissolved the tension in my chest, and I could cough freely and felt whole again. A show of anger will usually knit my divided self. Only afterward did I realize that the lightning flash to which I had awakened revealed the Son of Frankenstein in the labor of his twisted maternal passion, striking out the legend in his father's laboratory, so that it would read, instead of Maker of Monsters, Maker of Men. I smiled and fell asleep almost at once, remembering a little girl I once saw (on another television screen) whose father was a delegate at the United Nations. No more than five or six, she tapped her finger on a table and said in a voice as true as a bell: "It is necessary for the nations to get out their rage. It is absolutely necessary."

This morning my pillows were drenched with sweat, and I felt I had slept a week. Then I remembered the dreams. They had come in a series, much like the old horror films themselves, each dream shocking enough to wake me. In the first, I had discovered a bacterial culture of some kind generally believed to contain thirty thousand future human lives. I turned it over to a hospital laboratory technician who was to cultivate it in a test tube. My discovery would justify my existence, or make up for some serious shortcoming. But a bitter disappointment followed. The culture was too old to be of any value. I awoke in misery, feeling responsible for thirty thousand lives. Then, in sequel dreams, I began a round of killing, waking after each murder. I committed matricide and infanticide. I killed our dog. I killed my husband. It seemed I would never stop killing, and each murder was committed in black hatred, followed by an agony of remorse.

All morning I have been lighthearted. Not once has my chest gone tight against the cough. In fact, I can scarcely remember what it was like. Everyone must have thought me pettish and fretful. I'm sure of it, for now Minna Jackson is going to be moved. Her mother has arranged everything quite discreetly.

The baby has been here with his sweet searching mouth. I am very awkward with him because I cannot shift my position without help. The nurse who brought him is a young Negro girl, and she stayed a while to help me. She flashed a bright smile. "You'll laugh about this in a few more days," she said.

He wears a shirt of thick muslin with the name of the hospital stenciled outside. It is as rough as a gunnysack against his new skin, but this is the traditional costume, I am told. Probably his skin is less tender than it appears. Probably a baby is wonderfully strong in many ways. I looked and looked.

How different this baby is from the one already tamed by a week or two of domestic life! No wonder he is thought to be so fearsome that, aside from his guards, only his mother is allowed to touch him. His eyelids have the thin translucence of Japanese rice paper, and a fine design of lavender veins flicker in them. There is no eyelash at all, and the nostrils too are hairless, almost polished, little hollows. His skin *179* is puckered upon a hand that has not yet learned to grasp. And all his body is beset with little incompleted movements, starts, frowns, mirthless smiles. Every impulse seems to work in him like something he is learning without knowing any use for it. Even when he sucks, it is for a short, experimental span.

What most impresses me is my infant's eye. It is not innocent, for that implies some impure counterpart that ruins, some predicament of good and ill. But his eye sees no design, and has not yet begun the awesome task, which still often baffles the adult, of sorting reality from dream. No doubt has ever settled even on the surface of those dark blue depths, no doubt of self, of love, of form. They would change nothing in this world, not even next year's building blocks. They are less impressed by what appears before them than the baby lamb. It is as if, in these few weeks before they can identify my own, his eyes will be living out some final cycle in the story of the race, and still look only on the vast shapelessness of a primordial world. The tissue that once webbed his fingers has long since made way, as has the tail quite early on, for his final human mold. But just after birth, the forest shadows linger in his eyes, even casting their grayness upon the whites. They have not yet made way for those shadows that seem to be in the nature of man, doubt and anxiety, though every other fiber of his being, from the high dome of his head down to his perfect foot, bespeaks the intelligence of his kind.

180

The nurse who came visiting in the recovery room is named Miss Bloom. Her eyes are quite expressive and as vivid a green as I remembered. She was here before the baby's visit and helped me then to walk to the door and back. She has just returned for a short time. She wanted to know, "Did you use the Zephiran?"

I said, "I clean forgot."

But then she looked so dashed that I regretted teasing her. I could never forget the use of Zephiran. Miss Bloom had instructed me about it with some care.

Zephiran is an elixir that prolongs life. It has a place on every mother's night table, in a covered silver urn. The lid is important, for it keeps out evil elements. Every morning, the maid from "central supply" uncovers the urn to see if it needs filling. It must always be filled, for the mother must anoint herself with it before each visit from her child.

The color of purple, I imagine rather like the woad ancient Britons found so potent, this thin liquid is applied to the mother's breast. The following special procedure is observed: First, the mother removes the top of the urn, placing it inverted upon the table so that no foreign body will attach itself to the underside and enter the Zephiran when the lid is replaced. Within the urn, drenched in the elixir, are swabs of cotton. The mother bathes each breast with a different cotton piece, rotating it from the exact center outward. With a third cotton piece, she wipes her

181

hand, taking pains to touch the elixir between each finger, dampening every crease of her hand. After each of these three steps, she carefully discards the cotton in the basket underneath her table. It is later taken out by a handmaiden and presumably burned. The mother then replaces the top of the urn, and lifts her hands above her head. This gesture signalizes the end of the ceremony, and indicates that she is now prepared to receive the waiting baby. Then, and only then, does he enter the haven of her arms.

My doctor has returned and ordered for me a device that was once a part of every mother's costume; but it has fallen into such disuse that scarcely anyone knows what to make of it. Only Miss Bloom has had the patience and imagination to figure it out. It is an abdominal binder, now probably believed to inhibit muscular resilience, which will brace my coughing muscles. There are—we counted them—twenty-four straps that are folded one upon the other. The result looks something like a mummy shroud. Perhaps the thing impressed us both somehow as a relic of tradition. I was thinking how women are no longer bound to, but may need to, use such relics. And then, in passing, I asked Miss Bloom if she thought I might begin to do the postpartum exercises suggested in the mothers' class. She said, "No, they're only for after a normal birth." At once she betrayed

an inward start, and conscientiously corrected herself:

"I mean, a *usual* birth. You'll have to wait a few weeks."

I laughed. It was a reassurance somehow. Miss Bloom is too well trained to be the prey of outmoded superstition, and yet her young mind has not quite cast out the witches' chant upon the heath: "No man of woman born . . ." Duncan, we'll make your birth all normal yet, just as we'll take the pain away from childbirth. We moderns will drag the tribe from the sacrificial fire—one good day.

There is a choking sob to be heard in the arena tonight, and the rustle of briskness outside as the nurses hurry to help. I believe it is someone in the room next door, but I am not sure it is a sound of pain. Perhaps the hour makes me fanciful. It is very late, very still. Suddenly there comes a gasping cry. It is stifled at once, not as if the woman weeping were ashamed but rather wanted privacy. Hospitals reserve no space for grief.

The latest occupant of the other bed has come in surrounded by a great many of the hospital staff, all of whom call her Betty Ann. The nameplate says "Mrs. Elizabeth Ross." She has a small, enthusiastic voice, and a great desire to learn all she can about her delivery, and then to tell and tell. Although her baby was born only an hour or so ago, she has used the telephone twice, each time telling all she knew. She is extremely active. Some of those who are with

her have urged her to rest, as if they know it is her
nature to overtax her strength.

Now the curtain has been pushed back, and I
understand why Betty Ann is so well known here. Her
husband in an intern, and she has told me she is a
nurse, and has taught obstetrics at another hospital's
nursing school. Her husband has placed a box of cigars
on a shelf inside the closet. She asked him, "Was I
very bad, darling?" Without answering her, he picked
up the telephone and told the operator to try him on
that line if he could not be found elsewhere. He is
apparently on duty. "I've got to go have breakfast,
honey. We're going to be busy today." She seemed to
want greatly to please him, and, stretching her hand
out, she repeated, "Was I very bad, darling?"

He merely patted her blond hair. "You were just
like all ladies, honey," he said, and left.

Betty Ann seemed not to mind her husband's un-
obliging answer, for she was intent upon getting at
the truth of something. From what she has told me
and from what I could not help but overhear, I realize what it is. In her obstetrics course she has strongly
advocated a version of natural childbirth. But apparently—like me—she has been unable to use it herself.
A friend of hers, one of the nurses present at her delivery, came by at last and told her what happened.
"Every time a contraction started, you'd tense up and
try to stop it. You know you couldn't help it, Betty
Ann. You were right to ask for something."

"I *asked* for sedation?" she cried. Yes, and afterward it was much easier for the instruments to be used. "Instruments! ... Even that." Betty Ann's voice quavered with disappointment. Not only was her idealism shaken but her faith in her own nerve as well.

Her husband, so brusque this morning, has come by to collect cigars now for the sixth time. Each visit, he gives out statistics: weight, temperature, amount of sedation, duration of labor before dilation, and so on, in a voice that is extremely professional.

Just before he went away this last time, she touched his arm, "Why didn't you tell me about the instruments, darling?" she asked.

He slapped his thighs in a decisive, standing-up gesture. "Because you were carrying on enough," he said. And then, in the same professional tone, "Honey, you were fine. I'll tell you the truth. I've seen lots of ladies a lot worse than you were."

Tom has been here to tell me that we shall be going back to the West Coast in the fall. He is full of plans.

My news is less agreeable. We are causing a bureaucratic scandal. A son may not bear exactly the same name as his father, unless he uses some suffix like "Junior." We must relent and decide upon a middle name, or the state totters. But Tom needs neither to conform nor revolt. He chooses *two* middle names, and in one stroke satisfies the state and gives the baby two other namesakes. There is no difficulty he cannot overcome.

Behind her curtain, Betty Ann was on the tele- **185**

phone all the while he was here, telling about her baby's birth. I asked my husband what he made of the passion all these new mothers have to tell and tell. He laughed and picked up this journal. "You just write it all down," he said. I hadn't thought of that.

It was Mrs. Dante I heard crying last night. She had just learned that her new baby is a Mongoloid. Two of the student nurses have been talking about it outside the door. "That poor woman. She doesn't deserve such bad luck." The nurses spoke in tones of pity, but my own response is a cold anger.

When life presents us with its sudden cruelties, it is often a reminder of our ultimate limitations. A footing lost, a cable snapped, a train derailed—and all the clarity of mind we possess can lie in a fruitless heap. It can be enough to make us doubt the value of clarity of mind to begin with. I remember Mrs. Dante's sweet spirit and her generosity when her rest was disturbed by my low threshold of pain. It is easy to feel sympathy for so compassionate a nature. But I remember, too, the way she stared at our god's eye and what she murmured, half unconscious, when they wheeled her in: "No more ... no more ... If I was a boy I'd be safe." She had not wanted this child, nor the last several children before their birth. But she was overruled by her own modesty, and doubted too strongly her own power to challenge authority. Like my neighbor, Mrs. Harris, she has stood by while her town, her neighborhood, and her very house crash down upon her head, rather than dare to save herself.

We might take a fatalistic view of this "bad luck" that has befallen Mrs. Dante, but only if we truly doubt the value of clarity of mind. It lay within her power to prevent this particular misfortune. And although I don't doubt for a moment that other hardship or tragedy might well find its way to her, she surely owes it to herself (and perhaps to the rest of us) to avoid what pain she can. Against our limitations, we can do little enough, but that little we must do. Otherwise, are we more civilized than certain "primitives" who prefer to let a child die rather than give it inoculation against disease? They deserve our sympathy, too, it is said.

The technician is wheeling a tray of medication about the circle, as she does at this hour every afternoon. My doctor has ordered a sedative that does not accommodate her schedule. The other day when she came by, she said, "You're an odd one," meaning (I hope) that my medicine came at an odd hour. She has passed me by again today.

Perhaps she has something there for Mrs. Dante, who still weeps in stifled little sobs. Among all the women on our floor, she alone grieves; the rest know a measure of joy. Who feels the sharper emotion? Sometimes I think we cannot feel our joy so strongly as we feel our pain. We are always prepared for joy by hope, so that it can never take us by complete surprise. We have no preparatory counterpart for grief, except long illness or war, and even there hope intervenes.

187

Every time I sleep, I awake with a sensation of sweet, unreal alarm. Is the baby here with me? Is he safe at my side? Waking, I can feel his presence. A worry prods me—perhaps I am obstructing his tiny nose. Can he breathe? And in the same moment the truth penetrates this waking state: Of course he has not slept here. The nurse took him away hours ago. And yet, his head has thrust against my breast, an elbow has nudged my ribs. Baby, I murmur, are you all right?

Once Betty Ann was looking at me curiously as I awoke, and she said, "Me too. I feel that, too." Betty Ann has, of course, given much more study to obstetrics than I, and she has now decided that a delivery at home would have solved the difficulties she experienced. We talked of the "adaptation of natural delivery for the sacrosanct American woman," and she agreed that the techniques she had learned (and taught) were probably inadequate. But she added that American women are conditioned to one thing that no amount of preparation and hospital touring can take the place of—the humble bathroom. "Some women simply can't function as well in a hospital as at home," she insisted. "Besides, neither the mother nor the child would suffer the sense of separation you and I wake up with." I wouldn't have defined it quite that way—a sense of separation. What I felt was the illusion of a presence, palpable, tender, infinitely vulnerable. It didn't quite fit into Betty Ann's theory, but if the baby had been near me from his birth I well might not have wakened with that dreamlike mixture, both joy and fear.

She sighed. "But of course, my husband's a doctor, and he'd never agree with me." She said that even though nowadays most unusual deliveries such as mine can be predicted in advance and technical problems of home delivery could be easily overcome, it would be too great a sacrifice of time for doctors ever to revert to it. I couldn't help thinking that if fewer babies were born, doctors might become willing to make a further "adaptation."

But whatever dissatisfaction Betty Ann may feel, a powerful knowledge constantly breaks it down. "I have a baby, I have a baby," she keeps murmuring into the telephone, over the long-distance wires, to parents and friends.

I have taken a walk around the arena, have joined two others in the motherhood dance, clad in the colorful robes of recovery, with paint upon my lips to show that I am soon to leave. The other two who made this ambulation, as it is called, were Mrs. Jackson and Mrs. Dante. I should not have thought there would be much common ground between them, but I was taken by surprise. For one thing, they both have deepfreezes, although Mrs. Jackson concedes that her family isn't large enough to warrant it. She said she had spent the last few nights before her baby's birth preparing dinners for her husband which she stored in the food locker. "All he had to do was warm them up, and yet every time I've talked to him he's just eaten out someplace. I wonder why we bought the damn thing." But there is affection in her tone today toward her husband. She is eager to repossess what is hers: the freezer, the washer (even without the dryer), the station wagon, the man.

Today her discontent is submerged enough to make way for something else. She told Mrs. Dante she had been brooding about her handicapped child. There was, she said, a case in her husband's family. Pale and haggard, Mrs. Dante seems to have less energy than in those first few hours after delivery. She answered Minna Jackson's questions freely. Yes, she is apprehensive about the effect of this child upon the others. And Mrs. Jackson spoke with sudden heat: "I couldn't do it. I simply couldn't live with such a thing. I think you have terrific courage."

But Mary Dante seems to know she will hear such solacing compliments many times, and takes no credit. She is heartsick, but doesn't pretend that she is brave. "I wouldn't know what else to do," she said. And then I saw that Mrs. Jackson wanted to make a suggestion to her, based on the experience in her husband's family, and she spoke with such tact that I thought again I might have misjudged her. It is just possible that Minna Jackson may be enough disturbed by all the things she cannot own to have come in possession of a saving discontent.

Thoreau once said that the reformer is saddened not by his fellow in distress but by his private ail. Is it just possible, then, that the private ail, even a silly one, can be turned to some sweet use? Implicit in what Minna Jackson said to Mary Dante was a certain social outrage not unlike my own. If she feels that, then it is only one more step to seeing her own responsibility. What could make it plain to her, I wonder, that she herself has already had children enough? Our world, of course, does not encourage restraint. It still pays bounty for babies. I shall ask Minna if she doesn't think parents should be taxed for having more than two children, rather than rewarded with exemptions. While she is brooding, I may as well see if she can receive suggestion as graciously as she offers it.

I was just beginning my second ambulatory turn when the nursery sentinel arrived with her announcement. "The babies are coming." She flashed around the arena with a quick light tread, her brown eyes glowing as she called into the mothers' circle. Down the hallway, visitors stopped, hesitated, then took cover in a visitors' room, to wait until the babies had come and then once more returned to their lair. From where I stood at the white arena counter, I could study the strategy of their advance, all close together, side by side, united. On wheels. They have a contraption of canvas that ensures their safe passage, and each baby has his own cockpit. It fits about his body as strong as a sling, and is linked to all the others with a sturdy metal frame. The vehicle is convoyed by two dark women, watchful of eye, who send into confused retreat any lingering outsider. On they come without a hitch, the babies, every man jack raising a hue and cry.

I should not have stayed outside, but should have withdrawn, as Mrs. Jackson and Mrs. Dante did, to my glass box. But the desire to steal a look at all of *191* them was strong in me, and so I lagged behind, hoping no one would notice. But Mrs. Jackson saw me as she left, and smiled. "You're going to get caught," she said.

Get caught by the babies? I remembered my bewilderment that day last fall when the brown-eyed elf had stopped to warn me: *The babies are coming.* What did it mean? Was there some danger in them?

People who study other living creatures see a relation between appetite and custom. ("You *are* what you eat," Mrs. Drummond once declared, fixing me with a gimlet eye.) The carnivore is slow to get his bearings in the world. The tiger cub eats only what flesh his mother stalks for him, while the day-old lamb is so advanced that he can stand upon the grass he will eat and see the flock he will belong to. The tiger has no flock, and once he goes, he goes alone. He is the fearful solitary of Blake's poem, which reminds us of our own dual nature. That band coming at me down the hallway was both tame and unspeakably fierce. Its members will go alone as well as in a pack. They will eat of the lamb's green fare and of the lamb as well. The newborn human, like the tiger child, would be utterly defenseless, left alone. But his mouth is ferocious. His cry is terrible. He knows neither dread nor mercy. I have seen him close, and am afraid.

While I stood there, taking my close look at that infant train, I realized with a start something about my own baby. He lay in his bin, unattended. The nurses had gone off to deliver two of the others, and so I was safe for the moment in my defiance of the rule. My baby lay there, those little impulses starting in his face and flickering out before any meaning could be attached to them. And then his mouth suddenly flew open like the mouth of a sunfish reaching upward for a water nit. But, finding only air, it shut, his limbs stiffened, his hands hardened into fists, and his lips separated again to issue an unmistakable command. He's hungry, I thought, and was already halfway to my bed. Quick, uncap the Zephiran; quick, hold up your hands and give the sign. "Oh, give him to me, quick!" I cried. "Can't you see he's hungry?"

My baby has had his fill. He has lain in my arms for a few quiet minutes, his eyes open only to that early world before mankind, satisfied, all unaware that his appetite has stirred a harsh memory.

I saw quite sharply a three- or four-year-old boy digging in a refuse heap next to the city slaughterhouse. That was a common depression scene in our southern town. Every day the hungriest, both black and white—unsegregated—found their way to the dump. The boy had found a prize, someone's cast-off wishbone.

I had suppressed that ragged child for years, and am eager to be rid of him again. Push him aside, the world is bright. We have our handicap of plenty to consider, the choosing of a pattern for our lives. We want it to be beautiful.

How hard it is to sustain belief in hunger! Ap-   **193**

peased, it becomes something unreal. It is difficult to imagine the twenty percent of the earth's hungry human life, just as it is difficult to believe in the existence of hungry Americans nowadays, though we know they exist. We do not doubt those who tell us that in generations we may live to see there may not be food enough even for Americans, if the human race continues at its present rate of increase. We do not doubt that the nations could go to war for so simple a thing as grain or space to grow it in. We do not doubt, but we appear not to believe, either. Can that be because of the intervention of hope? Or is it because we are already cynical about the value of human life? We have often seen demonstrated the robust human gift for regeneration, and so perhaps after all we are expendable—in war, famine, pestilence. . . .

I know that at the time I saw the boy with the wishbone, my parents, like many others, were protecting me from hunger at the expense of their health. It is what parents do when they can. But sometimes they cannot. I wonder how that feels. The boy with the wishbone—what did his mother feel? Or the European Jew who watched her infant grow too weak to cry for food? She was hungry herself. It is said that hunger numbs adult emotion. Perhaps in growing used to her own agony, her child's starvation, too, gradually became a fact she did not feel. Everyone is quiet in a famine, not just the young lambs.

Happiness surrounds me today like a tide. I am
awash with gratitude. I want to make speeches of

thanks to everyone. I think there can be no better doctor in the world than mine. He has come at seven Sunday morning to see if it is safe for me to leave. His formal academic style returned as he talked to me of intimate things, because he knew that Betty Ann was listening behind the curtain. That increased my affection for him, but also placed some constraint upon my speech of gratitude.

No matter. Outside, there is a clear blue sky. The nurse who has just taken my pulse remarked that her hand was probably cold upon my wrist because she has just come inside. Cold? Well, a colder day than the last few have been. But still a spring day, brisk. Our baby's first day out of doors should be brisk and clear, I thought.

When I came here, I brought a handbag with a blanket and an infant dress and diaper. They were only several pieces of cloth to me then, and now there is magic in them. I have spread them on my bed and fingered every piece. They will be used today. They will be worn!

I shall leave shortly after two o'clock—in half an hour. Mother has just arrived, still rather ill but unwilling to miss the going-home ceremony. She is down the hallway looking at her grandson, before the babies are wheeled into the arena for the two o'clock feeding. Tom has gone for the car. Soon he will be able to touch his son for the first time, and take him home.

Home? Our infant will give up his life here with his own kind, forego his canvas cockpit, discard his stenciled muslin shirt in favor of the soft batiste my mother stitched by hand, and he will begin this thing called family life. I still wonder at it—receiving blankets, diapers, rattles—will all that heady disorder really be our portion?

We did not send for the Mexican cradle, but have instead an ordinary crib from Sears. It was the line of least resistance to buy this American thing with no exotic charm at all. But it is practical. And we have our god's eye to hang above it. Perhaps it well may ward off some antagonistic demon and help to keep us safe.

The time has come. Here she is now, the nursery elf, flitting down the hallway into the arena, to bring her tidings of danger and delight: *The babies are coming! The babies are out!*